*Friend of
the Library Donor*

Donated by
Terry Bales
SCC Faculty Member

© DEMCO, INC. 1990 PRINTED IN U.S.A.

THE TODAY SHOW

AN ANECDOTAL HISTORY

Gerry Davis

QUILL
WILLIAM
MORROW
NEW YORK

Library of Congress Cataloging-in-Publication Data

Davis, Gerry, 1949–
  The Today show.

  1. Today show (Television program)   I. Title.
PN1992.77.T6D3   1987   791.45′72   86-18006
ISBN 0-688-06766-2
ISBN 0-688-06545-7 (pbk.)

Printed in the United States of America

First Quill Edition

1 2 3 4 5 6 7 8 9 10

Book Design by Richard Oriolo

To my husband, Shep,
and sons, Mark and Clint,
and to my parents and brother . . .
whose encouragement has
never faltered

ACKNOWLEDGMENTS

Many thanks to those who took the time from their hectic schedules to contribute personal anecdotes and photographs. And to Steve Friedman, who said "go for it" and was always available with words of advice. Thanks, too, to the NBC Photo Department, Gary Grossman of *Entertainment Tonight,* and Frank Gregal, a *Today* show intern. Also to Lisa Drew, editor, and David Means, editorial assistant, who got and kept everything in place, and to Julian Bach, for his quiet, succinct words of wisdom.

"This is *Today* . . ."

These three words, heard at 7 A.M., January 14, 1952, were to usher in a new dimension in television and change TV viewing habits forever.

Thirty-five years later, January 14, 1987, with approximately 9,100 shows aired, *Today* has the unique distinction of being the longest running morning television show. It is the uncontested champion in total broadcast hours, numbering approximately 18,200, and is second only to *Meet the Press* as the NBC network's longest running commercial show. *Today* has become a television institution, often imitated, but rarely equaled.

After watching the Thirtieth Anniversary Show, Tom Shales of the *Washington Post* said in his column: "I couldn't help wondering, again, why anybody would tune in anything else early in the morning. *Today* is the first and still the best of the network news and talk shows."

It is hard to believe now that there was a time when there was no morning TV. Television was not something with which you started the day. Reception was provided by a pair of rabbit ears and if you turned the set on, you saw a test pattern.

It was the fifties, an era that many of us cannot talk about without first uttering a sigh and feeling a rush of nostalgia. Douglas Miller and Marion Nowak in *The Fifties—The Way We Really Were* wrote: "Domesticity, religiosity, respectability, security through compliance with the system, that was the essence of the '50s." Many might consider that decade bland by later comparisons, but that's only because they were not around then.

In 1952, Harry S. Truman was president and Alben W. Barkley was vice-president. A loaf of bread was 16¢, a gallon of milk was 97¢, and a pound of butter was 86¢. The average annual income was $3,850 and a new home could be purchased for under $10,000. A new Ford cost $1,754 and gas was 20¢ a gallon. The New York Yankees beat the Brooklyn Dodgers in the World Series, and Troy Ruttman achieved a new record at the Indy 500 with an average speed of 128.922 mph. The Dow Jones Index was 270.80. An ounce of gold was $35, silver 90¢, and copper 25¢.

Duncan yo-yos, Wiffle balls, Slinkys, Buddy L trucks, plastic models, and painting by numbers were all fifties fads. Reddi Wip became a household staple. But with all that was coming into

people's lives, no single event or item influenced humanity as much as television.

In any language, TV is TV.

It was a recreation. It was a form of entertainment, an escape. It was also an information center. People could now pursue a hobby—sewing, drawing, knitting—even play checkers or Monopoly while they were fed information. They didn't have to read anymore. Before, they would gather around the radio and have to be relatively quiet to hear the program. Now they could talk, listen, watch, and have fun while this new home accessory was on.

But initially TV was strictly an after-hours entertainment. No one turned on the set to start the day.

This was to change very shortly.

In 1949, when a 6-foot 4-inch Dartmouth graduate arrived for work at NBC, little did the network or, in fact, the world realize what this very creative, outspoken, unconventional man was going to do for the industry. But Sylvester "Pat" Weaver would become one of television's most creative executives whose innovations, profound understanding of the medium, and keen eye for talent has since been felt by millions.

Pat Weaver had an idea for a morning television show. Its format would be similar to a newspaper—viewers would be able to see and hear what had happened overnight. There would also be interviews with newsmakers and celebrities as well as presentations of timely interest—fashion, cooking, inventions, and so on.

Weaver felt that this new magazine of the air should not be broadcast from a studio but should be viewed, as it happened, by the public. It was decided that the storefront featuring RCA's latest television sets (the RCA Exhibition Hall on West Forty-ninth Street) would be home base for *Today*.

Insiders were to refer to this new endeavor in broadcasting as "Weaver's Folly," but like Seward's Folly and Fulton's Folly it was going to prove to be anything but.

From now on it would be possible not only to hear the news but also to see it—to see people, places, and things. People were not going to have to wonder if someone was short or tall, or blonde or brunet, or if countries or towns were congested or barren.

With all the positive aspects of television there were negative ones as well, the saddest being that our imaginations were going to be put on hold. Everything that we had had to visualize while reading a book or newspaper or listening to the radio was now going to be shown to us. The inauguration of a new era in media was taking place.

This visual factor was obviously going to influence who appeared on television. No matter how articulate a radio broadcaster might be, if there was no special audience appeal—a charisma, an attractiveness, or an awareness that could be perceived on the screen—that person was not going to make it as a newscaster in this new medium. Like movies during the change from silents to talkies, we were now going through a change from audio to audiovisual.

With these qualities in mind, the producers and staff of Weaver's Folly began their search to find the host for their new morning show.

T-DAY

Dave Garroway, too, was tall, six feet two inches, a large-framed man who wore bright, usually bow ties, horn-rimmed glasses, and argyle socks. He was a jazz buff and a car enthusiast with a large vocabulary, who would often use the most erudite word in the simplest sentence. His on-camera presence—timid yet direct—reflected total relaxation and sincere interest in what his guest was saying. He also had a sense of humor.

A former page at NBC and a graduate from the NBC announcers' school (where he received a very low rating from his instructors) Garroway's ease and talent at reporting events was soon recognized. Before long he was covering special events for the Pittsburgh station KDKA. From there he moved to Chicago's WMAQ where A. A. "Abe" Schecter, NBC's news chief, realized Garroway's talents, extended his projects, and began sending him on special assignments. Garroway's unusual observations and descriptions of events brought him wide attention, and within a short time he had a successful show in Chicago.

Dave Garroway's association with the *Today* show began with a fortuitous incident. One morning, reading a copy of *Variety,* the trade sheet of show business, he saw the front page article announcing NBC's new morning show. Dave was convinced he was the man for the show. He proceeded to convince his agent, William "Biggie" Levin, who in turn had to convince Pat Weaver. Mort Werner, the first *Today* producer flew to Chicago to meet and interview Dave. The two hit it off immediately, but that did not guarantee Dave would get the job. Within a few days, Dave was called to come to New York to read some hard news. He did so and then returned to Chicago, still not knowing his future. A couple of days later, he was told he had the job.

T-Day, as Weaver called it, was a cold winter morning. For two weeks a loyal and energetic staff of people had practiced, planned, and possibly dreamed about what they were going to tackle inside the RCA Exhibition Hall. For this group Weaver's Folly was going to become a reality, and for them there was a pervasive aura of excitement that only a premiere can generate.

There were not many hours of sleep enjoyed by the staff during those weeks. At 3 A.M. the night before the first show, producer Mort Werner was waiting for a cab. A policeman approached him wondering who would be up at this hour. Werner identified him-

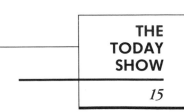

self, saying he worked for NBC and "We're doing a new television show starting today at seven o'clock." To which the policeman replied, "Television at seven o'clock in the morning? You must be out of your mind!"

By six, all cast and staff members had assembled. A fifty-minute dry run was scheduled. It took place, but it could have been fairly described as a rehearsal for total confusion. A few curious onlookers had assembled outside the window of the RCA Exhibition Hall. Perplexed at what they were viewing, they withstood the cold and watched as television history enfolded.

Five . . . four . . . three . . . two . . . one. . . . The countdown had started.

Dave Garroway:

❝ **Well here we are, and good morning to you. The very first good morning of what I hope and suspect will be a great many good mornings between you and me. Here it is, January 14, 1952, when NBC begins a new program called *Today* and, if it doesn't sound too revolutionary, I really believe this begins a new kind of television.** ❞

The first show was anything but tight, but it was a start. Dave Garroway was called the "Communicator." He loved electronics and gadgets, and in the first show he referred many times to the awesomeness of the TV equipment.

There were telephone hookups to London and Frankfurt that produced not much more than a "Hello" and "Good-bye." There was a remote from Washington that was provided by then Washington Bureau chief Julian Goodman (later to become NBC president). The viewers saw empty parking lots filling with cars, and a reporter stationed outside the Pentagon was seen asking the Chief of Naval Operations, William Fechteler, "How's the Navy going these days, Admiral?" To this the admiral replied, "Guess it's all right. It was there last night when I left it." "Thank you very much, sir," said the reporter. Then he continued, "Ladies and gentlemen, you have just heard from Admiral William Fechteler, Chief of Naval Operations down here at the Pentagon in Washington. And now we return to Dave Garroway in New York." In spite of this, the Washington Bureau was to become a vital and integral part of *Today.*

Also on the first show were Fleur Cowles, who was interviewed about her new book, *Bloody Precedent,* and Bill Stern, the sports commentator.

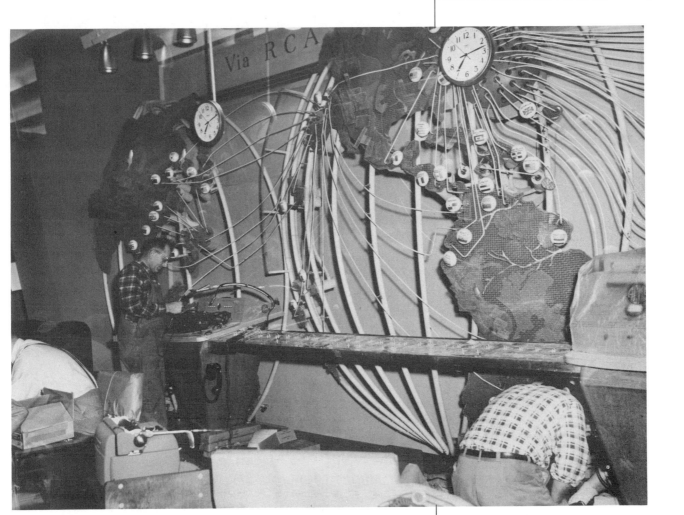

Getting ready for T-Day

Mobile units picked up early-morning scenes in Chicago and New York's Grand Central Station. Two soldiers in Korea were seen and heard as they spoke with their families who had been brought to the New York Communications Center.

Front pages of various morning newspapers were shown and excerpts from ten new records were played. Dave Garroway called the U.S. Weather Bureau on the air to obtain weather reports from around the country.

It would not be long before the *Today* show guest list would read like a *Who's Who* as well as a "Who Might Be." *Today* went out of its way to obtain the best guests for the show. There was no doubt that the spontaneous atmosphere and the sincerity of the interviewer, occasionally mixed with humor, helped guests to relax and say things that they perhaps would not reveal in more constrained surroundings.

The critics were anything but enthusiastic. From the first reviews:

The Today *studio, Dave Garroway at the desk*

. . . an incredible two-hour comedy of errors, perpetrated as "a new kind of television."—JOHN CROSBY, *New York Herald Tribune*
. . . something without which TV can do very nicely. . . .—JANET KERN, *Chicago Herald American*

But from the viewers outside the RCA Exhibition Hall there was applause, which supported and underscored what Pat Weaver and all those involved with the show so firmly believed.

Within a few weeks of the first show, a new routine was established, the three-ring circus effect was organized, and a format and purpose developed. Critics and viewers were realizing *Today* was here to stay.

Sonia Stein wrote in her review of *Today* in the *Washington Post,* "This is the week little Willie will be late for school and big Willie will be late for work 'cause TV has infiltrated the early-morning hours."

Dave Garroway:

We are going to try very much to put you more clearly in touch with the world we live in by this magnificent unparalleled means of communication which NBC has assembled into a single room in New York.

Viewing that first *Today* show with its potpourri of people, cameras, wires, clocks, newspapers, microphones, equipment, lights, and more lights one could only join Dave Garroway in his feeling of awe that anything even resembling a show could result. No one tripped or stumbled and Weaver's Folly, *Today,* did get on the air. The secret was that within this confusion of cables, lights, cameras, telephones, gadgets, there were creative characters, people who realized the awesome dimensions and potentially limitless parameters of what they were attempting to create.

Marie Finnegan (early staff member):

When the *Today* show started, we could be anything we wanted to be. It was a wonderful feeling. If we had an idea, we would suggest it to the producer, Mort Werner, and most of the time he would let us do it.

Once, I had gone out on a story on a day when it was raining. I had to go to Chinatown to line up some people for the show. I remember it was Chinese New Year. There were crowds and firecrackers— and I'm afraid of firecrackers. I said this is not what I want to do, so I went back to the office and on Monday I suggested that from now on I take care of the commercials. As I said, we made our our own jobs. I was there for over thirty years. **"**

Dave Garroway was *Today*'s "Communicator," but he had a supporting cast who helped make it all work.

Jack Lescoulie's words, "This is *Today*," not only ushered in a new concept in television, but for himself, a fifteen-year career with *Today*. He was announcer, sportscaster, interviewer, kidder, and "saver." The term *kidder* was derived from Jack's tendency to joke. Everyone enjoyed it, so he incorporated his kidding into the show and it worked. As for "saver," that was a description Dave gave him for his ability to "save" interviews. Jack knew when it was time to step in and rescue a bad interview.

Jim Fleming read the news, and a young woman named Estelle Parsons was the first *Today* Girl, a term that was to be applied to the girl *on* the show. Originally, Estelle's task was to telephone the U.S. Weather Bureau and obtain the most up-to-date weather information. Although on the set, she did this off camera. She would then transfer the information to Dave's weather map with red chalk. Red did not show up on the cameras of the early fifties, so when Dave gave the weather report he would trace over the red with white, which would be visible to the viewer.

It was not long before more of Estelle's talents were put to use, however, and her role on the show was enlarged. Soon she was seen chatting with Dave on camera and interviewing prominent guests.

Estelle Parsons:

❝ It's really funny when you think how people now scramble to get their face on *Today*. At the time of the first show, we discovered nobody wanted anything to do with it, because nobody would watch it.

I remember having so much trouble booking fashion guests. Givenchy was the only designer I could get and that was because he was just starting out.

The *Today* show was my first job in New York. I

Frank Blair

enjoyed it. It was what I did. It was a very exciting and pioneering time in television, but I was doing it to make a living till I could get into the theater. 9

Estelle Parsons was to play a historic role in television's coverage of politics as the first woman to go out on a political reporting assignment. During the 1952 presidential primary campaign she was assigned to follow Senator Estes Kefauver.

Estelle stayed on *Today* until 1954.

In 1953, Frank Blair joined *Today.* He was to stay with the show until 1975. It was his task to deliver the news to the waking audience.

Dave Garroway:

6 For details on the story as it stands right now at this moment, and for the whole news picture, here is that news editor —handsome Frank Blair. 9

Frank Blair:

6 I started in broadcasting in 1935, but I didn't get to work at NBC until 1950. One of the reasons I went there was that they had an idea. Television was just coming in at that time, just "a-borning," as they say. William McAndrew was then general manager of the NBC station in Washington (he later became president of NBC News and re-vised, rebuilt, constructed the whole NBC news department as we know it today). He had an idea that he wanted to put on a two-hour program on the local Washington NBC station from seven to nine in the morning. In those days television didn't go on the air until afternoon. The morning was just un-touched by television. They consulted me, then hired me to emcee this program, but, in order to get it going, the plan and the budget had to be submitted to New York headquarters. Well, they turned it down.

About a month later *Variety* came up with a story that NBC was thinking of an early-morning network program to go on the air seven to nine in the East-ern time zone starring Dave Garroway. Well, that

knocked me out of the emcee slot. Except that Bill McAndrew in his fairness said, "Well, you know, that failed, but now you're working for us." Then when the *Today* show went on the air on January 14, 1952, I don't know whether somebody in New York felt duty bound or what, but they named me the Washington correspondent. We had a lot of originations from Washington on the program—interviews with congressmen, senators, and V.I.P.s in general. That was the start of it, and I did that for thirty-nine weeks.

In the meantime, the first newscaster on *Today*, a fellow named Jim Fleming, stayed with it for twenty-six weeks. Then Merrill Mueller, whom we affectionately called "Red," got the nod and he stayed with it for thirteen weeks. That brings us up to September 1952. When Merrill decided he didn't like the hours and so forth, they yanked me kicking and screaming out of Washington up to New York, and I started then as the newscaster and stayed there for what turned out to **,** be twenty-three years.

The original *Today* was definitely a man's world, although the *Today* Girl was, year by year, to become more prominent and important on the show. The prerequisites for the *Today* Girl were that she be attractive, talented, and witty. Besides that, she had to be feminine, fashion conscious, food wise, family oriented, and, if necessary, able to pour tea! What she could *not* be was sensuous or sexy—that was not proper for the breakfast table.

When Estelle left, Lee Meriwether became the *Today* Girl.

Lee Meriwether:

" I loved working on the show. When I joined *Today* it was a culture shock for me. I had just finished the Miss America tour, where men are not really allowed in your life and you always had a chaperone at your left elbow. On tour, interviews were done in hotel lobbies or specified rooms but not in your room. Suddenly, I was doing a show where I got up at four A.M., worked with twenty men and eventually a chimpanzee. Dave, Frank, **,** and Jack were great. They became my family.

Jack Lescoulie:

❝ There was a great rapport between Garroway, Blair, and myself. It was a wonderful experience. ❞

Frank Blair:

❝ Because we were in this experiment—we considered ourselves unique—there was a great comaraderie throughout the whole office staff. We were constantly changing, trying to feel the pulse of America. ❞

Lee Meriwether:

❝ Dave had that wonderful way. If things went one way, well that was fine, if it went another way, well that, too, was all right. He was casual, easy, he went with the flow. Frank Blair was much the same way. Jack was funny, warm, witty. They were this marvelous triumvirate that suddenly became a quartet. Everyone brought out the best in one another. ❞

Today's *enthusiastic window audience*

Neither rain nor snow nor sleet kept the street crowds away. The Exhibition Hall on West Forty-ninth Street was a window on the world. People felt they were part of the *Today* show and often they were.

Occasionally Dave Garroway, Frank Blair, or Jack Lescoulie would interview someone in the crowd. Signs were often displayed sending greetings and messages either to the cast or to home viewers. A favorite incident was when a daughter wanted to show her family out West the progress of her pregnancy and profiled herself to the camera.

The concept of *Today*'s window was an innovation that provided a more personal and immediate ratings system than Nielsen could ever offer.

Lee Meriwether:

❝ I think I had a crush on Dave, Frank, and Jack. They were very protective of me. I had lost my father just before I went to Atlantic City [for the Miss America Pageant], and now I had three. Of course, they didn't like the fact I thought of them as fathers! **"**

As with any television show, the studio crew was vital. In the early days when television technologies were just developing, oftentimes one would learn by instant on-the-job training.

Fred Lights (stage manager):

" I'm from Chicago and when I came back from the war, Chicago was just Garroway crazy. To my amazement, when his radio show came on at dinner time at my home, you couldn't talk. You listened. And then, when his television show came on, he was like a god—to black people especially. It was just fascinating. I never thought I'd meet the man in person.

I was living in the Bronx, and I worked at NBC. They knew I was restless in my job and they would send me on different interviews. One was to observe the new *Today* show. One morning, the twenty-third of December, 1953, I was standing there

Dave Garroway, Jack Lescoulie, Frank Blair, Lee Meriwether, J. Fred Muggs

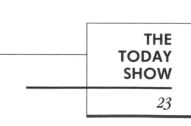

Fred Lights, stage manager

observing, and this fellow who was stage manager, Bob White, said, "Here." At that point he took off his headset and put it on my head and left; he'd quit. That's how I got to be stage manager.

I don't believe I moved from that spot the entire morning. I was in shock. I couldn't even walk. It never occurred to me that they were going to give me this job. The next day was the Christmas show and Mr. Garroway was off, so Jack Lescoulie hosted. I did the show by myself. . . . I wish I knew how many wrong things I did. But I stayed seven years.

Lee Meriwether:

We had freedom—we were not locked into horrendous formats. In those days we were responsible for putting on our mikes. They were large Lavaliere-type things with metal neck hoops. If you had to go to a place where the mike couldn't reach, you'd have to take it off, but then you had to remember to put it back on. If you didn't you'd be talking in dead air and Fred Lights would come over quickly and put one on you. We played this "Mike Game." If Jack forgot his mike we would go over and cut his tie as punishment. One time I forgot mine, and they got the scissors and made a big thing out of what they would cut off me. They decided they could cut a lock of my hair. Dave, holding up the lock, asked, "What am I bid?" They had calls and calls, and I think they finally sent it off to charity with a picture.

Over the years *all* major sporting events have been covered on *Today,* but in 1953 *Today* had its own sporting event, the First Annual *Today* Hole-in-One Tournament. It was held at Chicago's famed Tam O'Shanter golf course. Among the participants for the prize of $25,000 were Julius Boros, Walter Burkema (1953 PGA champ), Jim Turnesa, Earl Stewart, Jr., Dave Douglas, and Skip Alexander. When informed that the players would have to be on the links at six A.M., many commented, "For twenty-five thousand dollars, I'll get up at three A.M."

The *Today* Hole-in-One Tournament became an international happening. There were six foreign entries: Robert Vincenzo, Argentina; Hassan Hassein, Egypt; Yoshiro Hayashi, Japan; Herman von Nida, Australia; Carl Paulsen, Denmark; and Italian, Swiss, and Moroccan champion Ugo Grappizoni. The $25,000 prize was for a hole-in-one. Additional prizes were: $2,000 for the golfer placing a ball closest to the pin on the sixteenth hole (shortened for competition to 160 yards); second closest to the pin, $1,000; third closest, $500; fourth, $300; fifth, $200; sixth, $100. All those coming within a circle of twelve feet in diameter would receive $25 for their efforts. It was also determined that each golfer would be allowed two shots. The ball placed closest to the pin would be the one scored. However, if a golfer made a hole-in-one on his first shot, he would still be allowed to take his second shot, making it possible for him to score two aces for a doubling of the prize money.

It was an exciting event. "Babe" Zaharias, famed woman athlete who was recuperating from a serious illness, also joined the participants. Dave Garroway moderated the event from *Today* headquarters in New York.

Although thirty-six top-name golfers participated, none was able to claim the $25,000 prize. Jay Hebert, pro golfer from the Kahkwa Club of Erie, Pennsylvania, claimed the $2,000 prize for placing a four-iron shot three feet, nine inches from the sixteenth pin.

What was and is morning television? To some it is the sole contact with any world outside their immediate one. To others it is an extension of the newspapers. To still others it is entertainment—or a way of obliterating the noise of over-energized youngsters. President Lyndon B. Johnson said that watching morning television, particularly *Today*, kept him in touch.

It has been said that morning television often makes a great deal out of nothing. Others say it is nothing but a lot of noise, and some have been heard to say in disgust, "How can you start the day with that stuff?" Yet there is no doubt for many millions of people that *Today* is a morning habit, a way of life that begins their day in which the myriad elements of contemporary living are dissected and presented to viewers for their acceptance or rejection.

Regardless of one's personal feeling toward morning television, it is a very serious business, run by big business. Ratings and profits are the bottom line.

Frank Blair and girls

Pat Weaver:

⬤ By our mail we knew we were doing very well with the audiences, but we were still have trouble moving the show with the advertisers. We developed a trick where we would take the mail unopened, dump it on the possible buyers' desks,

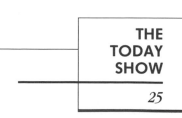

Dave Garroway and Win Welpin, commercial producer

and just say, "Open the mail. We haven't opened it. See what the people think. We don't care what you think, we don't care what the agency thinks. That's what you guys are supposed to worry about, the consumer."

So they'd open this mail and there would be letters thanking us for letting them see Washington, that they'd never expected to meet so-and-so, and it would just be gush, gush, gush. These guys would sit there and read the mail and they gradually got the idea and began to buy time on the show. **❞**

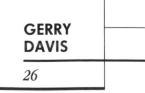

GERRY DAVIS

THE MUGGS ERA

By the beginning of 1953, *Today* had a dedicated audience. Instead of being seen in thirty cities, it was now reaching forty cities; rural America was also tuned in. Morning habits had changed forever. We were now eating, dressing, talking, and cooking while the *Today* show was giving us information and showing us people, places, and things. We were not just watching for fifteen minutes at a time as Pat Weaver had originally thought we would do. According to a poll, men were watching for forty-five minutes and women for fifty-three minutes.

But in spite of the audience's attentiveness, *Today* was strug-

J. Fred Muggs

gling. Advertisers were not impressed, and the show's forty-four sponsors were not enough to make it a money-maker for NBC. It was a crucial time for *Today.* If Weaver's Folly was to stay on the air there could be no monkeying around—or could there?

Enter J. Fred Muggs, a monkey. Who ever would have thought that a cavorting, diaper-wearing monkey would be the answer? But he was. Owned by Carmine Menella and Roy Waldron, two former NBC pages, J. Fred Muggs was introduced to producers Dick Pinkham and Mort Werner in late January. The events that followed made television history. J. Fred Muggs, ten-month-old chimpanzee, was put on the show the next day. After his introduction, press coverage was heavy. Children heard of Mr. Muggs and set the channel selector on *Today,* anxiously awaiting a glimpse of their favorite morning personality. Parents who for the past year had not turned on the TV in the mornings were now turning on *Today,* thanks to their children and Mr. Muggs. Ratings soared. Would advertising? That was the real question.

Joe Culligan headed *Today*'s advertising sales force.

Joe Culligan:

❝ We turned from a loss of $1.7 million a year to a profit of $2.4 million on a gross of $11 million on the first full fiscal year. ❞

Morning TV was a strange new concept for the advertiser, but they were soon persuaded to try it out. Before long Dow Chemical's new product, Saran-Wrap, was a morning advertiser. Dave Garroway would demonstrate the product, holding it up for viewers to see how clear it was. A perfect product for morning TV: A housewife, cleaning up after breakfast, realizes she can save leftovers with this new product. She goes out and buys it, the advertisers are delighted, and so is the sales department of *Today.*

The trade sheet *Billboard* said that *Today* was "probably the largest-grossing venture in the history of show business within a period of one year." On paper, in plain black and white, it was "an obvious" that advertisers' money went much further on *Today* than it did reaching the same number of people in the evenings on prime time. In 1953, a sixty-second commercial on *Today* cost $3,861. In 1986, the same slot cost between $12,000 and $19,000 per minute.

For over four years, J. Fred Muggs was part of *Today.* Dressed in his familiar little-boy attire, Muggs would sit on Dave Garroway's lap or on the desk and "converse" or "act-up" depending

"The perfect product for morning TV,"
the original Saran-Wrap box used in
the commercial on Today

on his mood. Although it looked as if Muggs had complete freedom while on the air, he was usually on a leash held securely by one of his trainers.

Luckily, J. Fred Muggs turned out to be quite smart and clever. He understood several hundred words, could mimic and cavort, and over the years he learned what the red lights on the tops of the cameras meant. It indicated which camera was on and "on" Muggs went, having figured out that he was never spanked when a red light was on him. Smart chimp.

Upon occasion Muggs caused a few calamities, but his popularity and earning power were more than many Homo sapiens'. West Africa was his birthplace, but America became his home. J. Fred Muggs became an integral part of morning TV, for which *Today* and NBC would be forever grateful.

Lee Meriwether:

❧ **One time we were all going on a remote— Muggs, too. We got on the plane, and Muggs was seated next to the window, his trainers in the next two seats. I was in the row in front on the aisle, so I could look back and see Muggs. Well, we took off and as we banked into the sun, Muggs was looking out the window, squinting his eyes, and I swear to you, he reaches up and pulls down the shade! No one had told ❧ him. He was just so smart.**

As a *Today* star, Muggs for four years traveled the United States and received tons of fan mail. He skiied, ice-skated, waltzed, sung, played the piano and the drums, all to the delight of *Today*'s viewers. He showed off his comedic style with Bob Hope, Phil Silvers, and Jackie Gleason—not to mention his daily solo ad libs and monkey shines. As Muggs "matured" so did his rambunctiousness, and, without much to-do, it was announced in an NBC News release that J. Fred Muggs "has decided to terminate" his association with *Today* in order to "extend his personal horizons."

Dave Garroway:

❧ **Muggs has broken up more than one show and taken the pressure off long hours of telecast-**

J. Fred Muggs "reading" the morning news

Averell Harriman being interviewed by Joe Michaels and Paul Cunningham

A "cushioned" Muggs ice-skating with Lee Meriwether

ing. It will be a different world around the set without him. We all wish him well. **9**

Today later tried to replace J. Fred Muggs but soon discovered that the original Mr. Muggs was irreplaceable.

Fred Lights:

6 There is something I would like to get off my chest. Many people say unkind things about J. Fred Muggs. I defend him. Muggs was not a trained circus animal and he was used to being loose. Muggs was cute when he was a little baby, but he got strong as he got older. By the time he was three or four he could take Lescoulie's desk and pull it all over the place. This began to frighten us. But it wasn't his fault. The trainers would tell people to relax and let him come to them, but they wouldn't do this. Basically, Muggs was gentle and friendly. He certainly was not vicious. He just got too old and strong and hard to control. He didn't know his own strength.

After Muggs was off the show, I went to New Jersey, where he and his trainers lived. They took me down in the basement. There in this massive cage was J. Fred. It was the first time I had ever seen him without his clothes! Seeing that he had to be behind bars was heart-wrenching. He had grown so much. 9

On March 15, 1954, *The CBS Morning Show* aired from 7 to 9 A.M. with Walter Cronkite and Charles Collingswood heading the news team and Jack Paar acting as host. It was the first real competition for the *Today* show. But because *Today* was so well established, *The Morning Show* never really worked. CBS turned to the wonderful Bob Keeshan, Captain Kangaroo, to fill the 8-to-9 slot, which he did admirably for over twenty years. But the valuable 7-to-8 slot was still open. A variety of talk-show hosts was tried, including Dick Van Dyke and Will Rogers, Jr., the son of the humorist, who took over from Van Dyke. The hour took the form of unprepared variety.

There is no question that Dave Garroway was at the right place at the right time. He was a skilled television performer despite the fact that in front of a crowd or at a staff meeting he was almost monosyllabic. He was intelligent, a super salesman, friendly to his TV viewers, quiet and given to understatement, and he was The Boss. He even had a private bathroom installed in his office. He would do almost anything to avoid a confrontation, and if someone was to receive a pink slip it usually arrived when Dave was out of town. A man of no describable talent, such as dancing or singing, he was still a consummate performer, who could hold the attention of his viewers and relate to them in a very special, intimate way.

"Peace." Why did Dave Garroway utter "Peace" at the end of every show? Because it had been his sign-off to radio and TV audiences since his Chicago broadcasting days in the forties.

"Peace," Dave said, "is a word that has been used as a farewell and also a greeting for many centuries. It has no superstitious meaning for me. It's just something I started to say, and it has been my trademark ever since. When I came to television and said, 'Peace,' I raised my hand—which also, by the way, has been a universal symbol of peace for generations. On the desk in my office you'll see a small bronze hand raised with the palm forward. It happens to be Buddhist, but the same symbol means peace wherever you see it."

Dave Garroway: "Peace."

Jack Lescoulie:

❝ The hardest part of the show was filling in and dreaming up what ❞ to do on slow days.

Fred Lights:

❝ Jayne Mansfield was to be on the show and Jack Lescoulie agreed to do a scene from Shaw's *Caesar and Cleopatra* with her. They had rehearsed it. But then a big news story broke—the *Andrea Doria* sinking. With all that was going on, that woman worried us to death. It was as if she was oblivious to everything else. Major disaster or not, all she could think ❞ of was the exposure.

Dave Garroway placed a glove with money on the sidewalk. Will anyone pick it up?

The era of the "ism" was born in 1957 on *Today*. It happened this way:

Dave Garroway suggested at a staff conference that more "anecdotes" be included on the show. But then he hedged about the word *anecdotes*.

Jayne Mansfield and Jack Lescoulie:
Caesar and Cleopatra

"They're not exactly anecdotes," he said. "Let's call them bits."

"Why not Garroway-isms?" someone suggested.

Garroway modestly shunted that idea aside. "Let's call them just plain 'ism,' " he said.

Then someone asked Dave for an example of an "ism."

So he told a story about a man who rented a safe-deposit box in a bank. The man put a fresh mackerel into the box, and then left for parts unknown. Before too many days had passed, the stench grew unbearable. But the bank was in a quandary. Legally, it had no right to remove the mackerel, yet the situation demanded action.

"It's not a ha-ha joke," explained Garroway. "It's just an 'ism.' "

"It sure is!" commented one staffer. "Sadism!"

In 1956, Helen O'Connell replaced Lee Meriwether.

On June 17, 1958, *Today* covered the "inside story" of the new $25 million American Flag passenger liner *Santa Rosa*, built by

Newport News Shipbuilding. In order to prepare for the telecast, members of the *Today* production staff boarded the ship at Newport News, Virginia, and put the final touches on program arrangements as the ship sailed to New York.

Jack Lescoulie was cruise director for vacationing Dave Garroway, and Frank Blair delivered the latest news "on deck."

Reports included a description by Captain Frank Siwik of the first "gyrofins," purported to "reduce ship roll by as much as ninety percent." Viewers visited the ship's dining room, which accommodated all three hundred passengers in one seating. A fashion show was presented aside "the largest swimming pool afloat" and songs were sung by Helen O'Connell from the huge promenade deck.

In 1958, Betsy Palmer joined the show. Betsy was very much like Lee Meriwether in that she had a special sparkle—even at 6 A.M.—and a genuine naïveté that was a delight.

S.S. Santa Rosa

Betsy Palmer:

❝ It was very much an ensemble team. We all sort of took over for one another in those days; I always knew I was loved on that show.

Jack Lescoulie always took the brunt of jokes and experiments. One morning we were doing a thing on Isaac Newton—like Ernie Kovacs did, where there was always a camera trick involved. Jack was talking about Newton's gravity and he goofed it up royally. I looked at him and I said, "Oh, Fig Newton!" He broke up.

And so the morning went. We never ❞ knew what was really going to happen.

Betsy was on the show for only six months. She was an actress and felt that because the show was a full-time job, if she stayed on, she would not be able to pursue a stage career.

In 1958 it was alleged by a rival television manufacturer that RCA was unfair because its products could be seen on television in the RCA Exhibition Hall.

The storefront Hall, which had been *Today*'s home for six years, subsequently lost its prestigious morning show. Despite sentimental attachments to their showcase, Garroway and Gang moved to the new and enlarged Studio 3K in the RCA Building.

Betsy Palmer:

❝ When we were in that fishbowl on Forty-ninth Street, it was very interesting. For one thing, we had an audience. They were always there, waiting to hold up their signs. We could see them, and we could see what the weather was. We could "see."

Very magical things could happen on Forty-ninth Street. We were not isolated and we became involved because the audience was. The producers were flexible in those days. That was the glory of live TV—it was not a dress rehearsal, it was like life. When we went into the third-floor studio, all of a sudden it was like losing the air. ❞

Fred Lights:

❝ There were advantages to being "in the window." We didn't have any real scenery, but we always had people or the outdoors to shoot if we needed a picture.

When we went into the studio everyone was excited because now we would have so much more scenery and facilities. Well, at the end of the two hours the first day, we had about thirty seconds to get ready to repeat the first hour. No one had thought about a replacement for the window. We had nothing to shoot. You should have seen the shock, the chaos, that first morning in the studio. It looked like the chariot race for *Ben Hur*. The first thing that was done after that show was to get a fish tank as the replacement for the window. ❞

Studio 3K was one of the most modern in New York. With its expanded facilities, additional direct lines, special electronics, and new technical effects—such as rear-screen projection, animated and other background effects, and special lighting—more elaborate staging was now available. There was also "sponsor space" for live commercials. Scheduled features of the first week in Studio 3K were:

Actor and musician Jackie Cooper presented his jazz sextet.

Cliff Evans, *Today*'s sports editor, on a remote from Municipal Stadium, Baltimore, previewed baseball's All-Star Game.

Thirty debutantes, on their way to the first American Versailles

Debutante Ball at the Palace of Versailles to aid the palace restoration fund appeared, as well as Gypsy Markoff, playing the accordion.

Dave Garroway had a magic potion that he called "The Doctor." No one ever truly knew what its ingredients were, but it was green.

Fred Lights:

❧ My father was a dentist, and when he came to visit the show he watched Dave drink something. Dave usually called it "The Doctor." My father could see Dave's reaction to it. Then I watched Dave, and it certainly ❧ wasn't good for him.

Frank Blair:

❧ Occasionally Dave would say, "Anybody like a sip of The Doctor?" or something ❧ like that, but not too often.

Betsy Palmer:

❧ Dave took some sort of green stuff in the morning. He took things to get him to go to sleep and to wake up.
   He collapsed in my arms one morning, just before we went on the air, when I was ❧ sitting between Dave and Jack.

In October 1958, Dave Garroway, who had been at the helm of *Today* since 1952, was felled by what doctors called "physical exhaustion." *Today* would be without its Communicator for a month. It was not until November 24 that Dave, swinging a cane and wearing a homburg and a broad grin, returned to *Today*. Everyone was delighted.

As the show began, Dave noticed a large calendar on the back wall. The pages had not been changed since the day he left, October 23. He reached over and tore page after page off, and a typical Dave Garroway monologue took place. He recalled what he had and had not done during the previous month.

Dave Garroway:

❝ I've missed you. Been away a long time. But I got a lot out of the past month. I got to know my children. I met my wife again, and I didn't meet myself coming home. I read a lot of books I never thought I'd get the chance to read and I found out something really important to me. I did a great deal of nothing. I filled up my days with nothing and I found then that I wasn't cut out for "noth-inging"—and so let's get back to work. ❞

As the years went by, the responsibility of *Today* began to get to Dave. He became suspicious, he spoke of poltergeists and spirits; the Communicator's emotional health was in jeopardy.

Today had reigned supreme for six years. Bob Bendick, who was now producer, realized that Dave needed a rest from the early-morning schedule. It was decided that *Today* would "go to tape," taping the next day's show in the afternoon, but leaving slots for live news. Excuses were made—taping would resolve union problems, taping would allow more guests to appear on the show, and so on. There was no mention of Dave's problems. *The New York Times* announced TODAY BECOMES YESTERDAY. "Going to tape" was a mistake that lasted almost two years.

In the meantime, Charles Van Doren, teacher and intellectual observer, had become *Today*'s resident professor, joining the show in October 1958. He had gained immediate stardom by winning big money on CBS's quiz show *Twenty One,* but then he was accused of cheating. *Today* backed him openly. Investigations continued while Van Doren gave reassurances that his answers were all given according to Hoyle.

Up to this point, January 1959, pessimism about *Today* had been pushed aside, the gamble had become a sure thing, reviews were raving. It was the seventh anniversary of *Today.* Over the previous eighty-four months there had been many comings and goings under the leadership of bow-tied Dave Garroway. The supporting cast had remained fairly constant. Jack Lescoulie, who was on hand as Dave's "right hand" from the first, remained as sports editor and funster. Frank Blair, news editor who had joined the show in 1953, stayed on.

The contents of the 3,360 *Today* hours had been impressive in every way. Countless governors, congressmen, top-ranking military figures, and people in the news from all walks of life had gotten up at four or five in the morning to be on *Today*. In-depth reports had been presented and for overnight happenings, such as the sinking of the *Andrea Doria,* the sudden death of King George VI, and the dramatic rescue of trapped Nova Scotia mine workers, *Today* had been there.

THE
TODAY
SHOW

Remote van in Paris

TODAY ABROAD: A PARIS VISIT

The first *Today* trip abroad was to Paris from April 27 to May 1, 1959. Availability of mobile videotape equipment and jet transport allowed the show to be recorded in Paris—in five different neighborhoods—flown to New York, and played the following morning. Although primitive by contemporary technological standards, the 1959 "remote" to Paris was the beginning of many *Today* odysseys.

Dave Garroway, Jack Lescoulie, and Charles Van Doren were the hosts for the event. Different French woman acted as the *Today* girls during the Paris remote. Frank Blair remained in New York to do the live news inserts.

Dave Garroway:

❝ I'm glad *Today* is taking the initiative toward international television, and, at the same time, international understanding. We can go anywhere now—Rome, Moscow, the Sahara Desert. ❞

Producer Bob Bendick had surveyed the Paris project's possibilities months before. With the facilities of Intercontinental Television's specially built equipment, a custom-built thirty-five-foot land cruiser that contained three RCA TV cameras, two videotape recorders, and special audio and power-generating equipment that would accommodate a wide range of special effects, *Today* could present its first overseas remote.

The taping timetable was as follows: Friday and over the weekend, Monday's show would be completed and flown to New York for broadcast on Monday. By Monday, Tuesday's show would be finished and sent back, and so on throughout the week.

The first Paris show was an exciting happening for *Today* and the television industry, not to mention the wonder and enjoyment derived by viewers. From the Champs Elysées, to Saint Germain des Près on the Left Bank, to the famous restaurant La Tour

*Dave Garroway, Jack Lescoulie,
Charles Van Doren, and audience in
a Paris café*

*Dave Garroway and Brigitte Bardot at
the Eiffel Tower*

d'Argent, the *Today* viewer once again was sharing a first with *Today*.

Although the Paris remote was a television success, viewed by enthralled audiences, soon thereafter, Charles Van Doren confessed he had been coached on the quiz show and that his winnings had all been a sham.

The morale of the staff plummetted as ratings and viewer enthusiasm escalated.

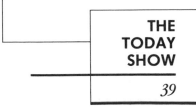

INTERVIEWS

From its inception, news was the keystone for *Today,* but the program was also the arena for expressing views, debating ideas and introducing people, objects, gadgets, appliances—even places. In spite of background preparation by the writers for the cast, the spontaneity of a *Today* interview always created the possibility of surprise. Neither the cast nor the audience was ever quite sure what was going to happen. That sense of the unknown was and is what makes live TV so special. No one believes anything that is too perfect. A taped show is as near perfect as you can get. A live show is real—like life—with its highs and lows, bloopers and successes, lost spots and unexpected confrontations. When we watch a live, unrehearsed interview we can empathize, revel, cheer. It allows us to become part of the show.

Florence Henderson recalls a humorous experience she had when she was a *Today* Girl in the sixties in "an interview with a Japanese lady who did not speak any English":

She had written a book on floral arrangements. We were sitting before the cameras when I asked my first question: "What is your book about?" She smiled and did not answer. Then I asked if she could show us some pictures in the book, and again she just smiled. I now knew I was in trouble.
I was just going to have to get through it the best way I could. I opened the book and carried the segment myself. The stage crew thought it was a riot.

What was Dave "The Communicator" Garroway really like? From all reports he was unique.

Estelle Parsons:
Dave Garroway was an immensely gifted man, one of the very few in television. I always and the greatest admiration and respect for him.

Betsy Palmer:

❝ I learned to interview people by watching David. He and Jack Paar, I think, were the finest interviewers because they both listened. Dave pointed out to me once, "You have a script and you go with the questions, but you listen so that if something catches you and you want to go with it you'll have been listening and you can go with it." I used to watch him and I learned an awful lot. ❞

As the "Communicator," Garroway was a master, though unorganized, peripatetic, and skilled at taking you totally off guard.

Beryl Pfizer (now an Emmy-award-winning NBC News producer) was one of the *Today* girls, and in 1960 became a regular on-air member. She recalls Dave Garroway:

A two-hour program takes lots of planning and setup so that everyone in the studio knows what to do next. We followed a routine that lined up news, guests, commercials, and features. Dave's favorite sport was to decide he should move the guests from the second hour into the first hour. And so, what had been a well-organized plan for a program dissolved into a whirlpool of frantic producers, writers, TelePrompTer operators, propmen, and technicians all trying to undo and redo their work in time for air.

The actress Vivien Leigh had agreed to a rare television interview while she was appearing in a play on Broadway. I met and talked with her before the date and prepared some questions and an introduction. I thought Dave would be caught by her charm, as everyone was who had seen her as Scarlett O'Hara in *Gone with the Wind*. When the live interview began, he read the introduction, then looked her in the eye and asked, "Miss Leigh, if you lost all your hair, would you wear a wig?"

During the eight months Beryl was on the show, she kept notes daily. Here are some of her entries:

Dave tells a story about renting a car in Mexico. He parked it. When he came back, he found tire tracks on the roof. He says an airplane must have bounced off it.

DG says he has put microphones in the gargoyles in front of

Dave Garroway, Jack Lescoulie, and "Today Girl" Beryl Pfizer at the Today *desk*

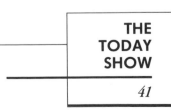

his house on Sixty-third Street so he can listen to people plotting to break in.

DG says you won't believe this, but between the time he left home and got to the studio, someone or something turned his undershorts around: they're on backward now. [Beryl Pfizer:] I don't believe it.

Florence Henderson:

❝ He was a very funny man with a keen sense of humor. He always said *Today* was more fun than a barrel of monkeys, and to prove it, he had someone bring a barrel full of monkeys on the set. It both terrified and amused me to watch the little creatures running around, jumping from light fixture to light fixture. We received a lot of letters; people seemed to really get a kick out of it. ❞

Jack Lescoulie:

❝ Dave Garroway was a personality. He would do his homework. He was good, but he was a personality, too. ❞

Frank Blair:

❝ I became a great admirer of Dave. The only sad part of it was to see the man change in the years he was with the *Today* show. I don't know what the reason was, but in the beginning he was one of the most delightful, charming persons I had ever known, and I relished the idea of being associated with him. As time went on in those years, Dave seemed to deteriorate, almost fall apart. Some said he had a drug problem, and we—Jack Lescoulie and I—were aware of that. He would take medication to get to sleep and then he'd have to take something to wake him up. It was the job. He was just tearing himself apart, and it changed his personality a great deal. ❞

Pat Weaver:

❝ On the *Today* show Dave Garroway became one of the first superstars of television. If you looked at the crew you saw all these different things going on, yet Dave was serene and calm and witty and charming working with the rest of the cast, handling the problems that always come up when you're on live television. Later he handled the bites when J. Fred Muggs would get out of control. Dave's serenity went right through the set. When he said "Peace" the crew probably all said "Peace" right back to him. He was really marvelous. 〟

One of the last people Dave Garroway hired was a young Sarah Lawrence graduate who had been at CBS. She admits she was a very nervous writer when she joined the *Today* staff.

Barbara Walters:

❝ In those early days we did a lot of fashion shows and a lot of what I call tea-pouring segments. Anita Colby had been hired to do five-minute inserts, and I was to write the material. It was a very different show. Frank Blair and Jack Lescoulie were on with Dave.

My first real assignment was to go over to Paris to cover a fashion show. 〟

Today's fashion firsts: flowers, ca. 1955

THE
TODAY
SHOW

43

Rome fashion show

TODAY *IN* ROME

In 1960, from April 11 to 15, *Today* went to Rome. Dave and Jack Lescoulie took the American viewers on daily tours that covered such famous areas as the Appian Way, Via Veneto, the Forum, the Colosseum, the Piazza del Popolo, and the Spanish Steps. Art, fashion, entertainment, history, and culture were all topics of reports.

Today received permission to take lights into the Basilica at the Vatican, and the show's final presentation from Rome aired in New York on Good Friday. It was devoted to St. Peter's Cathedral and the Vatican.

Peter Ustinov

After the Van Doren incident and Rome, *Today* made plans to go back to live. But live or tape, the pressures could not be eliminated. By 1960, Dave's condition had declined severely. His dependency on others and his insecurity on so many fronts were more prevalant than ever and the effect on the staff morale was acute. Pamela Wilde deConinck Garroway, Dave's second wife, whom he had married in 1956 and by whom he had a son, had been suffering from a nervous disorder.

Frank Blair:

❝ **After taping on April 28, 1961, Dave took his three-year-old son to his house in Westhampton, Long Island. They often did this, commuting in Dave's Jaguar. Pam stayed in New York. On April 29, Pam was found dead from an overdose of barbiturates.** ❞

Mobil unit at the Rome Colosseum

It was a dreadful tragedy and, on Monday, Frank Blair had to relate not only the tragedy but also explain that the reason Dave had been looking so relaxed was because the *Today* features were taped.

Although obviously shaken, Dave stayed on *Today*. However, his behavior became more erratic and extreme. One day while negotiating a new contract, as one story reports, he lay down on the floor and wouldn't get up unless his conditions were met. Dave's bluff was called and the first host and role model for morning TV, the eccentric Communicator, was relieved of his duties after ten years on June 16, 1961.

In 1962, John F. Kennedy was president and Lyndon B. Johnson was vice-president. A loaf of bread was 21¢ and a gallon of milk was $1.04. The average annual income was $5,556 and the average new home cost $12,550. A new Ford cost $2,924 and gas was 28¢ a gallon. The Yankees beat San Francisco in the World Series. At the Indy 500, Roger Ward drove 140.292 mph. The Dow Jones Index was 639.80. An ounce of gold was $35, silver $1.08, and copper 31¢.

In the early days, *Today* was actually three hours. The third hour was a repeat of the first so the show could be seen in the Midwest and West. Neither the NBC network, nor the industry for that matter, had the technology then to accommodate different time zones. Hence the East Coast's second and third hours became the West Coast's show.

As technologies improved the third hour was dropped, but the reversal of the first and second hours continued until 1979.

Without missing many beats, NBC News correspondent John Chancellor succeeded Dave Garroway. Although *Today* was already news oriented, there had been a strong emphasis on the scientific, the offbeat, the trips abroad, all of which reflected Garroway's eclectic interests. With Chancellor at the helm, *Today* was to take on a more direct news approach. But the most significant change after Garroway was the return to live broadcasts and, eventually, the move back to a window studio.

When Chancellor replaced Garroway, Edwin Newman replaced Frank Blair at the news desk, and Frank Blair replaced Jack Lescoulie. Thus began a reign of the bland threesome, a case of misplaced talents.

John Chancellor was on the show for a year, but his heart was always with hard news.

John Chancellor:

❝ I confess to having been very uncomfortable doing the show. After six months I wanted off and asked to leave. I was really grateful to get off, although I think being on the show helped my career. People saw me, and I got comfortable being on the air. It was useful to me to see the other side of broadcasting. It was an instructive experience. ❞

The succession also marked the return of Shad Northshield, who had been a producer during the Garroway reign. Chancellor knew Shad and requested him as producer. With this excellent bargaining chip, Shad negotiated a new contract and returned to *Today*.

Shad Northshield:

❝ When I did *Today* it was supposed to be a news show. We had Chancellor and Ed Newman to read the news and Frank Blair as announcer. We had a succession of "girls," and finally one named Barbara Walters. She was marvelous and she was a real reporter. ❞

Barbara Walters:

❝ Along with John Chancellor came Shad Northshield. He was terrific. He had known me at

John Chancellor and Allen Dulles

CBS and he said, "Whatever men can write, she can write." That was a big step for women.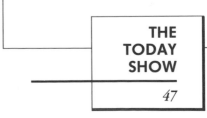

Shad Northshield:

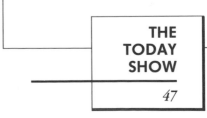 I certainly enjoyed the show. I remember once Barbara was able to get to Otto Preminger and she went out to do the interview. When she came back, she and I sat around the office talking about the segment when a huge box arrived. In it were a dozen long-stem roses and a little white envelope. Within the envelope was a metal part of a garter, which Barbara realized she had lost. Otto Preminger, being the perfect European gentleman, had returned it without any comment, but with a dozen long-stem roses. This was kind of characteristic of the mood of the place—lots of fun.

Barbara Walters:

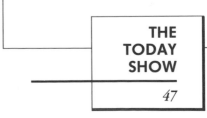 I was not a co-host. There was no such thing as a female co-host. In those days I began by doing my own interviews outside the studio. If it was a serious interview and it was done in the studio, it was automatically given to a man.

The first outside interview I did that was a breakthrough was with Dean Rusk. He had been secretary of state and had done almost no interviews during the whole Vietnam period. He had been a fan of *Today* and of mine. He had written me a wonderful letter which ended, "If any NBC vice-president gives you a hard time, show them this letter and tell them to leave you alone." When he left office, he was the first major interview I did. We ran it in three parts. It was a very happy time.

In 1962, John Chancellor and Shad Northshield both left the show.

John Chancellor:

 Leaving the show was one of those tricky things. I had not told Shad that I wanted to get off, or why. I went to see Bill McAndrew. I said, "We have

to close the door," and he said, "Close the door."
I said, "I have to get out of this, I'm going crazy."
The first question he asked was, "How many people have you told? Have you told your wife?" Yes,
I had. "Well, okay," he said, "but don't tell another
soul. Don't write it down, don't tell a soul because
I know the network business and you don't. They
may try to turn it around to make it look like they
are trying to get rid of you." Okay. "This is most
important," Bill said, "because it could hurt your
career."

Within a very short time, like the next week, Bill
comes down with hepatitis and was out for six
months. I stuck by my promise to him and didn't tell
a soul. When he came back, he asked if I had told
anyone and I said no. He said he'd get to it right
away. It took eight more months to get me out
gracefully. It reflects a little bit on life at the
networks. Bill was very wise on those things. He
worried about my welfare and he ❠
wanted to have a smooth transition.

In September 1962, Hugh Downs began with *Today*.

Hugh Downs:

❡ I did *Today* for nine years. We were in the Florida Showcase, which was on the ground floor
of the RCA Building, not where the show had originally been, across the street in the RCA Exhibition
Hall. The Showcase was set up with mannequins
wearing summer clothing, and there were displays
about Florida. When we arrived each morning, all
this stuff was cleared out and put into a kind of
dark storage room adjacent to where we broadcasted from. There was no outside window in this
room. It was kind of piled in a jumble and then
reassembled when we finished the show. I remember my first morning, it was about four forty-five.
The stage manager asked if he could get me some
breakfast and I said fine. Before breakfast I decided to go over my material in the storage room.
It had one light on. I was in there by myself rehearsing. I didn't realize that one of the things that
they had in the Florida Showcase were myna birds
in a cage. They, too, were put in this room with a
drape over the cage so the birds would sleep. All
of a sudden, thinking I was alone in this room—
remember behind me are the mannequins looking

GERRY
DAVIS

like they were in a freeze frame—this human voice suddenly comes out and says, "My name is Jungle Jim." I rose out of my chair and almost went through the ceiling. In a fraction of a second I realized it was the birds. But they gave me such a start that as a result I had a very high 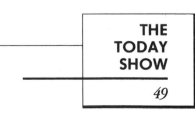 adrenalin level for that first show. 〝

From 1962 to 1969, Al Morgan was producer of *Today*. He felt that it was a marvelous job, and many remember Al as a marvelous producer.

Al Morgan:

Barbara Walters was a fine writer. We let her do the fashion pieces and occasional women's pieces. One of the first high points of her career was when she went to India with Jacqueline Kennedy. After that I began to use her on other assignments. I really respected her. She learned how to edit film, score a story, get the story on the air. I feel I raised Barbara from a cub. 〝

Barbara Walters:

You have to be very disciplined to work on *Today*. The hours are horrible. Pat Fontaine (a *Today* Girl) was a lovely person, but after a year on the show she found the schedule did not agree with her and she left. Al Morgan saw Maureen O'Sullivan and thought she was wonderful and made the mistake a lot of people make. They see someone do a wonderful interview and think that they can come on and do interviews. So with a lot of publicity he hired Maureen, and it was a disaster. Maureen left. While they were looking for someone else, Aline Saarinen, Judith Crist, and I were on. Little by little they went back to doing their specialties, and I stayed on the show.
I always thought I was enormously lucky. 〝

Hugh Downs:

When I first came on the show, there was a lot of turmoil because it had gone through a lot.

When Garroway left, John Chancellor was persuaded to do it for a year and he wanted to get back to hard news, which he did. But at the time of his departure I think there was a lot of confusion as to what the show should be. It took a little while—a few years—to shake down to where people were operating with maximum efficiency and to where people felt good about each other. **,**

Al Morgan:

❻ Moving a show the size of *Today* from its regular berth in the RCA Building to the remote corners of the earth can sometimes be as difficult as mounting an amphibious invasion—and will have the same casualty rates. I've lost staff members all over the globe to ringworm, malaria, the tourist trots, and airline hostesses.

I remember the time our remote unit—the size of a bus and a half—rolled off a tanker into the harbor of St. Croix in the Virgin Islands and knocked out every power line on the island.

I also remember a wet, rainy morning standing in the shell of the burned-out cathedral in Coventry, England. Carved into what was left of the altar was the legend "Father forgive them!" which had somehow survived the bombs and the fire. With us was a British photographer. He walked over to one corner of the cathedral and stood looking around silently. When I joined him, he looked up at me and smiled.

"It's funny," he said, "on the night of that fire bombing, I was right here, strapped into an antiaircraft gun shooting at the German bombers."

A lighting man named Vorst was passing. "You know where I was?" he said. "I was in a plane up there."

The two men looked at each other and shook hands, and you somehow had the feeling that whoever carved that motto on the altar knew what he was talking about. **,**

In 1962, a year after the death of her husband, architect Eero Saarinen, Aline Saarinen entered the world of television. In 1964, she was named an NBC correspondent. She had appeared on a number of NBC News specials and was hostess and moderator of WNBC-TV's *For Women Only.*

GERRY
DAVIS

Aline Saarinen's assignment for *Today* was to report on manners, morals, culture, and the arts. As a leading art authority and critic as well as author of a 1958 best-seller, *The Proud Possessors,* she was an outstanding addition to the show.

Watching *Today* as one dressed or ate breakfast had become a habit in millions of households. Thanks to Producer Al Morgan and the entire *Today* show staff, *Today,* as one reviewer stated, "is more than a good program, it's a necessary one."

By now numerous foreign dignitaries and many major American officials had appeared on *Today.* In 1964 alone, nine cabinet members made a total of fifteen appearances; forty senators made sixty-two appearances; twenty congressional representatives made twenty-nine appearances; seventeen governors made twenty-three appearances; and twenty-two other high government officeholders and department heads made twenty-four appearances.

Al Morgan:

I think one of the most exciting things we did was the inaugural telecast with the Early Bird satellite on May 3, 1965. I was in the control room in Brussels—everything was being fed into that room. Barbara Walters was in Paris with Yves Montand, Jack Lescoulie was in Holland, Aline Saarinen was in the Forum in Rome, Hugh was in Westminster Abbey, and Frank Blair was on the Capitol steps in Washington. We wanted to open with children in each of the areas saying, in each of the languages, "Good morning, this is *Today.*" It was the first time this had been done and it was very exciting. We had also arranged for the Pope to speak at this historic event. Our writer for the Pope's address, Bob Conniff, became known as the Holy Ghost Writer.

I'll never forget saying, "Cue the Pope!" I also remember being responsible for delaying the changing of the guard at Buckingham Palace by two minutes and ten seconds for the first time in the history of the British Empire. The order for that live broadcast by Early Bird satellite was this: We planned to open with a message from the Pope, cut from that to the most adorable little girls we could find saying "good morning" in their own languages from Rome, Paris, Amsterdam, and London, and go from that to the changing of the guard at Buckingham Palace. Unfortunately, the changing of the guard started straight up on the clock, and by the time we would be able to switch from the Vatican

to London we had no choice but to join the changing of the guard, which was, as they say, "already in progress." We pleaded with the Foreign Office, threatened to talk David Merrick into not importing any more British actors, and even offered the Queen a color kinescope, to no avail.

The night before the broadcast, we ran into an off-duty member of the guard in a pub. He was very excited. He had an aunt in Omaha who was thrilled because she would see him on TV.

"She won't see you," we said. "We're not going to do the changing of the guard."

"Keep it in, mate," he said.

We did, and on the morning of the broadcast while the Pope was reading his message, I saw on our London monitor the changing of the guard *not* taking place on schedule. I could see why. Our friend from the pub dropped his rifle. The officer finished chewing him out just as I said, "Take two," and we came up live from the palace as the ceremony began—two minutes and ten seconds late. **9**

Joe Garagiola, former major league catcher, sportscaster for the St. Louis Cardinals, play-by-play announcer for the New York Yankees, and game-show host joined *Today*. From the very instant Joe began on the show he was liked and admired by everyone, staff and viewers alike. Witty, affectionate, understanding, straightforward, Joe was another good addition to *Today*.

Joe Garagiola:

6 Working on *Today* was like a college education for me. You'd read about someone in the paper and the next day he was in the studio. Even if you were not the one who was doing the interview, you would get a chance to meet him and talk to him. The show did a whole lot of things for me. It allowed me to say something aside from home run, touchdown, and hocky puck. I'll always be loyal to it. **9**

Hugh Downs:

6 I suppose there are things I would have done differently. Yes, definitely. It's true that regrets are not what you have because you make mistakes. You don't usually regret a mistake. You regret what you didn't do. I've regretted things I didn't say.

In younger years, I used to burn inside because of a conflict between my image of myself and what I probably really was or am. Now I am much more comfortable with that. I don't have the great desire to have people see me differently than how they see me. I suppose every man may feel he's a swashbuckler at heart. You always want to give the snappy rejoinder. You wind up going through life with some awkwardness, but I find now that the awkwardness is part of life. It doesn't dismay me anymore.

Joe Garagiola:

I've seen people come in the studio who had been up all night for fear they were going to oversleep. There was one person who thought the show was taped and became very indignant and irate because we didn't hold the show for him.

Hugh Downs:

When somebody's a guest on *Today*, it's often a once-in-a-lifetime thing, and it's very important to him. To us it was just an everyday event; we had a whole parade of guests. As I look back, I really should have set up the machinery to write a personal note to every person who came on the show.

One never really knows how a live interview will go, but that is part of the charm and interest for the viewer and for the host. Some guests can take so long to make their points that by the time they reach them the alloted time is up, but those are among the hazards of live TV, where rigid time frames must be adhered to.

Joe Garagiola:

I was on the show the day Ed Newman asked George Jessel to get off. He and I were there

with Jessel doing jokes—I think about *The New York Times*—and old Ed just bounced him off. He thanked him and said, "I've had enough of this. The interview is over. Thank you, Mr. Jessel," and Jessel stood there with his fly open. Ed was great! **9**

Barbara Walters:

6 Probably the happiest time on the show was with Hugh Downs, Joe Garagiola, and myself. The chemistry worked. Each of us liked each other enormously. Joe had a saying that I never forgot —"There is no such thing as a good Amos and a bad Andy." We made each other look good and we played up to each other's **9** strengths. We were kind to each other.

Joe Garagiola:

6 Barbara, Hugh and myself really did have great chemistry. Of course, I have always been a Barbara Walters fan. She is a thorough professional, and Hugh was just unflappable, always under control, and that's what it takes. It comes through the tube—the chemistry. I know I felt it.

One day [former Green Bay Packer] Ray Nitschke came on the air. He is as bald as I am, and he was going to sell toupees. Well, before the show I see this guy with a head of hair and horn-rimmed glasses walking by me, and he says "Hi, Joe." "Ray?" I asked. I hardly recognized him. I said, "You can't go on like that, take that rug off." But he had one for me, too. So I said, "When you come on we'll talk just a little bit about football and then when we go to commercial break I'll say, 'Now you people don't go away, 'cause when we come back Ray's got a toupee for both of us and we are going to be two different guys.' "

While the commercial was on they rushed to fix us up. I could see what they were doing to Ray and he could see what they were doing to me. When we went back on the air and looked into the monitor, I looked down at Ray and said, "Ray, you look beautiful." Ray looked at me and said, "You look beautiful, too," and for three minutes these two gorillas sat there saying how beautiful they looked. People

Joe Garagiola, Barbara Walters,
Hugh Downs

couldn't believe it. I think that was the morning that General Gavin was on. He was running for the presidency. I think he later got fifty or sixty letters. But Barbara or Hugh had said something like, "I wonder what our viewers think—Joe with or without a toupee?" We got *thousands* of letters—"Put it on . . . Take it off . . . You look horrible. . . ." It was the biggest mail pull I ever saw. I said, "That's what's wrong with our country—people are more worried about my head than what General Gavin was talking about!"

Another time I was interviewing a priest. We said good-bye and he said, "Pray for me, Joe," and I said, "Me pray for you? You're in management. You ought to pray for me." It was just a flip remark. The purists got out their rosaries and were going to beat me within an inch of my life for being so sacrilegious. It was just a little throwaway line, but the audience reacted to it.

Hugh Downs:

One day a piano was being delivered to the show. I don't remember who the guest was, but a piano was needed. The piano people arrived, and a guy in coveralls presented the bill. The manager signed the bill and said, "You can bring it in now." The trucker's helper, who had arrived in another vehicle, said to the first guy, "Well, where is it?" to which the first guy said, "Don't you have it?" It turned out that neither of them had the piano. One of them had had it when he started out and no one knew where it had disappeared to. I remember saying, "Well, did you leave it in a phone booth or something?"

We got on the air, and I had some time to ad lib and told the piano story. I got more responses from that—people remembered it for years.

Joe Garagiola:

I had a terrible time with the word *startlingly*. I had to use it in a commercial—I think it was for some salad dressing. They had to write it out phonetically—start-ling-lee —like Chang Kai Shek.

Would you like to do another morning show?

Joe Garagiola:

❝ Yeah, now that my children are grown, I'd love it. ❞

Hugh Downs:

❝ I'd rather not. I did enjoy doing it then, but I'm now doing what I want to do, which is a multi-subject hour. I'd always aimed at that, ever since *60 Minutes* went on the air. I said, "God, I'd love to do a program like that." Well, now I'm doing it. That really closes the doors to daily stuff. ❞

Barbara Walters:

❝ I loved it. I was very happy on the show. But I would never go back and do another morning show. You know when I came here to ABC I was offered a chance to participate in *Good Morning America*, and I couldn't. I was so attached to the *Today* show that for the first two years, I couldn't watch it. I still love so many of the people. ❞

For the first time in *Today*'s thirteen-year history, major segments were broadcast in color on September 13, 1965.

The amount of turmoil, drama, and brutality that the *Today* show experienced, and taped, at the Chicago Convention in 1968 has never been surpassed in the United States.

Susan Butler Miles *(former production assistant)*:

❝ We were all at the Chicago convention in '68— Hugh, Barbara, Paul Cunningham [correspondent], and Joe Garagiola. I personally never went to bed. We got there Sunday night and we didn't stop until we closed the show on Friday.
We could not solidify the show until four A.M. We

were out all day getting stories. Guests were in and out. We had Jesse Jackson on the show and then Lester Maddox. They met in the hall. It was not-cordial.

We were all victims of [Chicago] Mayor Daley. I was hit by a policeman's billy club.

We had meetings in the middle of the night with the Yippies and with Abbie Hoffman.

About four of us lived in our production office. We were staying in the Hilton right across from the park where all the riots were going on. The McCarthy kids were getting all bruised and beaten by the National Guard so we brought them into the hotel. I remember Nancy Fields [production assistant] running around bandaging and helping them.

Aline Saarinen and Gabe Pressman were the reporters on the scene. Peace demonstrations were taking place across from the Democratic headquarters at the Hilton. Tear gas permeated the air. Due to a bus strike many of the hotel employees could not get to work. Hotel services were practically nil. The telephone system was overloaded with hippies and Yippies, police and press.

Susan Butler Miles:

We were sort of a traveling troupe, and we shared an incredible number of bad times— really awful experiences that brought us together. We had to handle world happenings such as wars and assassinations, and they brought us all very close. Love affairs were part of the deal. You'd switch from coffee to booze and back to coffee. We were always awake. It seemed like years of no sleep —lots of tensions and enormous amounts of fun!

After nine years, Hugh Downs left *Today* and Frank McGee replaced him. It was Al Morgan who had first brought in Frank McGee for the vacationing Hugh Downs. In spite of McGee's reputation in the NBC News department for being tough and heavy-handed, Al Morgan was pleased at how natural he was on *Today*.

It soon became apparent that Frank McGee's voice—stern but with Southern softness—did not reveal the real McGee. He was always outspoken, even in his youth, and very rarely apologetic.

Frank McGee , Frank Blair,
Joe Garagiola, Barbara Walters

After a stint in the army, Frank had returned to his native Okla-homa where he obtained a job at a TV station. He learned all aspects of television, and there was no question that he was good. NBC hired Frank and assigned him to cover the civil rights move-ment. He was the first to give national coverage to a young Baptist minister, the Reverend Dr. Martin Luther King, Jr., and to Rosa Parks, the weary black seamstress who refused to move to the back of a Montgomery, Alabama, bus, thus precipitating the Mont-gomery bus boycott.

In October 1971, the *Today* show cast was Frank McGee, Bar-bara Walters, Joe Garagiola, and Frank Blair.

Today show viewers soon realized that the new host resented Barbara Walters's abilities and, within a few months, tensions were evident from all angles and toward everyone.

Barbara Walters and Mamie
Eisenhower

In 1972, Richard M. Nixon was president and Spiro T. Agnew was vice-president. A loaf of bread was 25¢ and a gallon of milk was $1.20. The average annual income was $11,859 and the average new home cost $27,600. A new Ford cost $3,853 and gas was 55¢ a gallon. The Oakland A's beat the Cincinnati Reds and the Dallas Cowboys beat the Miami Dolphins in Super Bowl VI. Mark Donahue traveled 163.465 mph at the Indy 500. The Dow Jones Index was 950.70. An ounce of gold was $58, silver $1.67, and copper 62¢.

In twenty years a lot of changes had occurred. What had been the average annual income in 1952 was now the price of a new Ford. At NBC, *Today* was still number one.

Barbara Walters:

🌑 Frank never really liked doing the show. He felt it was a comedown. Although we all got along on the air, it was a very unhappy time. While Frank was there I was not allowed to participate in any of the Washington interviews. He wanted to do them alone. There was a big meeting with the president of NBC, and we finally compromised. I could come in and participate in an interview after 🌑 he [Frank] had asked three questions.

THE
TODAY
SHOW

THE TWENTIETH ANNIVERSARY

January 14, 1972, was a very special show, the Twentieth Anniversary broadcast. Remembering the comments of the critics and the skeptics in 1952 one could only gloat.

Success is never due to just one or two people and the success of the *Today* show is a perfect example of a "far-out idea" that became network TV's longest-running weekday program, thanks to a truly dedicated staff and an equally inquisitive audience.

On the morning of January 14, 1972, four of the program's hosts were on hand: Dave Garroway (1952–1961); John Chancellor (1961–1962); Hugh Downs (1962–1971); and the current host, Frank McGee. Jack Lescoulie was also present, as were *Today* girls Estelle Parsons (1952–1954); Helen O'Connell (1956–

Twentieth anniversary show: Jack Lescoulie, Dave Garroway, Frank McGee, John Chancellor, Hugh Downs, Frank Blair

1958); and Betsy Palmer (1958). Barbara Walters led the *Today* girls down memory lane.

Frank Blair reported not only the news of January 14, 1972, but also re-read the news of January 14, 1952. Paul Cunningham, who had been with the program from its start and was now its reporter-at-large, was on hand with a historic film of *Today*. He also presented a man-in-the-street interview, just as he had done in the early days.

According to the Nielsen survey in 1972, nearly six million people watched *Today* each morning.

Stuart Schulberg *(former executive producer):*

❝ **All I can say is that the first twenty years are the hardest.** ❞

In the summer of 1972, *Today* went to Miami Beach to cover both the Democratic and the Republican national political conventions. Frank McGee and Barbara Walters were the program hosts, along with regulars Joe Garagiola and Washington news editor, Bill Monroe. Daily dialogues by the sharp-witted William F. Buckley, Jr., and John Kenneth Galbraith were enjoyed by *Today* viewers. Politics were not the only topic of the broadcasts from Miami Beach. Regional reports and stories involving prominent sports figures and entertainers were also included.

In January 1973, *Today*'s resident Catholic, conservative, sportsman, Italian, "Tell it like it is" Joe Garagiola, left the show. A devoted family man, he felt the time had come to spend more time at home and on other projects.

Joe Garagiola:

❝ **It has been a pretty rewarding life, that's for sure. If it stopped tomorrow, I could only cry—I couldn't be bitter; it's been some ride.** ❞

Gene Shalit and Larry Grossman entered the doors at NBC in 1973. Gene Shalit had been at *Look* magazine. When Larry Grossman became NBC vice-president of advertising (he was later to become president of NBC News), he brought in Gene. The two

William F. Buckley, Jr., and John Kenneth Galbraith

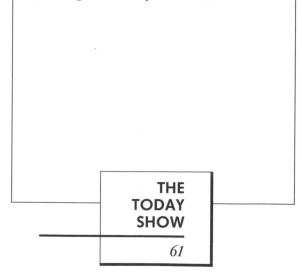

Joe Garagiola's last day on the show

had edited a book titled *Somehow It Works,* about the 1964 presidential election.

Larry Grossman:

❛ I suggested that the news division look at Gene Shalit for an all-night radio program. He began to do some work for them. He was a reviewer, and before long he began his career on the *Today* show. ❜

Barbara Walters:

❛ In the beginning, Gene had a tough time being accepted by the *Today* audience. I adored Gene and still do. He kept me going, and I kept him going. ❜

Larry Grossman:

❛ My first association with the *Today* show was when I held the lowest job on the totem pole at *Look* magazine in the promotion department. They called me to accompany the *Look* All-American Football Team around. The two main shows in 1954 were *The Ed Sullivan Show* and *Today.* The *Look* team was put up in the Hudson Hotel on the West Side, which was barely a respectable place then. In order to go to the *Today* show, one had to get up at five in the morning.

A Carey bus was arranged, and I was in charge of checking off all these guys. Dawn was breaking over New York. The *Look* All-American Football Team in full day-glo colors, with their monstrous pads and helmets and their monstrous-looking clothes, come parading out of the hotel, and here I am checking them off when I hear a groan from behind me. There was a drunk, who looked at these monsters in their crazy day-glo outfits and literally went up against the wall. He either stayed sober for the rest of his life or has never taken a sober breath since!

That was my first encounter with *Today.* ❜

The development of the Minicam (a small portable videotape television camera) made it possible to expand coverage and do reports from various locations.

Gene Shalit

A remote was scheduled with Gene Shalit in Times Square on December 16, 1974. There were heavy rains and winds that morning. A musical presentation by the Salvation Army Band and an interview with its members was planned. Cables from the mobile unit already had been laid out when a New York City Sanitation Department truck with sweeper and vacuum came through, sucking up the cables and detaching them from the truck. The cables were quickly adjusted, but then the generator in the truck failed. The engineers needed a substitute power source and found an outlet in a lobby of a building and plugged in—upside down—neglecting to ground the system. The ground was obtained by the cameraman, who was holding the wet camera with wet hands and standing on a wet sidewalk! When the current was switched on, the shock caused him to drop the camera. The cameraman and camera survived with only slight "denting," and the plug was corrected.

If the Salvation Army Band could stand in the rain for the interview, so then could Gene. He handed his umbrella to the unit manager, who hung it on the metal grillwork protecting a closed store behind them. As the interview progressed, there was suddenly a very audible crunching sound. The storekeeper had pushed the button to raise the grillwork and Gene's umbrella was rendered useless.

At this point the program blacked out. The building superintendent, walking into his lobby and noticing an unfamiliar line plugged into one of his outlets, pulled the plug. Finally, the Salvation Army Band struck up, only to be met with a stumbling and disgruntled Times Square character who demanded, "Stop the music! Too much noise!" When the segment was over, Shalit was asked what the chances were he would do another outdoor broadcast. He responded, "Remote!"

By the spring of 1974, Frank McGee's physical condition was deteriorating. Although viewers could not tell, it was obvious to all who worked on the show. In early April, he was taken to the hospital. On April 17, 1974, Frank McGee died of cancer.

Barbara Walters:

In 1974, Frank McGee had cancer. We all knew it, although he hadn't said anything. His last few months on the air were strange.

When Frank died, I was on vacation and immediately flew home. NBC announced that they were going to look for another host. Remember, I had now been on the program for eleven years. Obviously I had a contract. In it it stated that if Frank

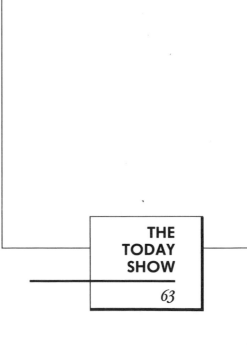

McGee left, voluntarily or otherwise, I would then be co-host. Frank McGee was a young man, and NBC never thought they would have to honor the clause, but when Frank died, they were forced to make me co-host. Ever since then, anyone who has come in has automatically become co-host on every morning show. And that's how it happened. ❞

NBC was now faced with finding a partner for *Today*'s first female co-host, Barbara Walters.

Barbara Walters:

❝ Everyone was on. Tom Brokaw was on. Tom Snyder was on. Garrick Utley was on. Jim Hartz was on. Everybody. People thought that Snyder and I wouldn't make it 'cause we both have hot personalities. The fact was, we were crazy about each other. ❞

Edwin Newman, the intelligent host of many NBC specials, and Douglas Kiker, the Washington news correspondent, were also guest co-hosts.

NBC News Press Release, April 22, 1974:

BARBARA WALTERS WILL BE CO-HOST OF THE NBC TELEVISION NETWORK'S *TODAY* PROGRAM FROM NOW ON, DONALD MEANEY, VICE-PRESIDENT, TELEVISION NEWS PROGRAMMING ANNOUNCED TODAY.

THIS IS THE FIRST TIME THE PROGRAM HAS HAD A CO-HOST, AND *TODAY* IS NOW THE ONLY TV NETWORK NEWS OR PUBLIC AFFAIRS PROGRAM TO HAVE A FEMALE CO-HOST.

It was not long before NBC announced that Jim Hartz had been chosen to succeed McGee. As it turned out, both Oklahomans were close friends, and McGee had been Hartz's mentor at NBC News.

Jim Hartz, thirty-four, with his boyish smile and open friendliness, had impeccable credentials for the *Today* show position. For the previous ten years, he had been the top-ranking anchorman of NBC's local newscast in New York. He had the ability to take very complicated technical issues and deliver them in a simple and clear manner. He also had a good sense of humor.

Jim Hartz:

There were a number of highly qualified newsmen within NBC who could have handled this assignment. To have been chosen from among such a group made the honor doubly meaningful and rewarding for me.

Working on the *Today* show looked like a very posh sort of deal. You'd be through by nine A.M. and you'd have the whole day free. But it never worked out that way. Everybody was always there till five or six in the evening. Then you'd try to hit the sack around eight.
It's terrible on families.

FOR IMMEDIATE RELEASE:

A kidney transplant operation was performed on nationwide television for the first time—live on the *Today* program this morning (Thursday, February 26) on the NBC-TV Network.

The operation was performed at Downstate Medical Center in Brooklyn, New York, by Dr. Samuel L. Kountz, professor and chairman of the Department of Surgery there and a pioneer in kidney transplantation. The patient was Robert Fuco of New York City; the donor cadaver kidney was flown in from Chicago. Dr. Frank Field, NBC science reporter, reported from the operating room. The telecast pointed up the great need for people to donate human organs for transplant.

Shown in [the photograph on page 66] is Dr. Kountz performing the surgery.

During 1974 and 1975, *Today* traveled extensively. To commemorate the U.S. Bicentennial *Today,* beginning July 4, 1975, and during a part of each week until July 4, 1976, saluted each of the states of the Union.

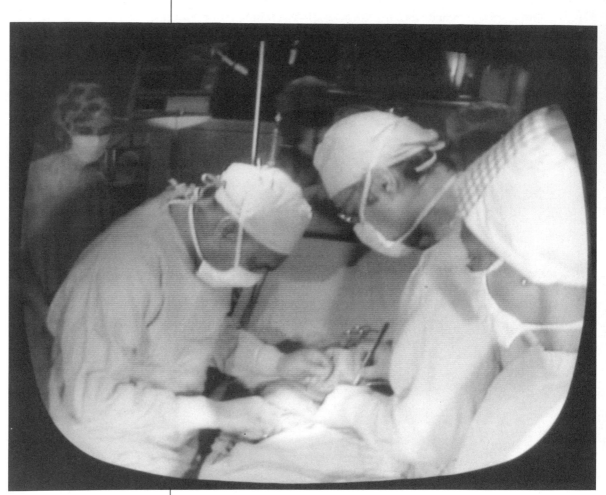

Dr. Kountz in action

Jim Hartz:

❝ In 1975, we began the Bicentennial series and we went to every state. The following year was an election year, and we did all of the presidential primaries. I think I traveled something like a quarter of a million miles during that year for the Bicentennial, the primaries, ❞ and the conventions.

It was a traveling year not only throughout the U.S.A. but outside it for the *Today* staff. Barbara Walters went to China with Nixon and Jim Hartz went to Japan. By then satellites had changed much of the world's communications.

Jim Hartz:

❝ We once had a guest who was a gal who had written a book about something like how to keep your husband. What this woman said in the book was that a wife ought to say every once in a while to her husband, "I crave your body." I don't remember whether Barbara or I interviewed her—or perhaps we both did—but she really got into that thing about how important it was to say, "I crave your body." That got to be a little private joke with the staff on the show. Everybody was going around for weeks saying that.

Later, when Barbara was in China and I was in New York, we were testing the circuit. The satellite always comes up ten or fifteen minutes ahead of time. Engineers' talk was going on. Finally they opened the circuit so that I could talk directly to Barbara in Peking and she could talk to me. I could see her. So when the circuit opened up, I said something cute like "Good morning" and yawned. Barbara has a great sense of humor that not many people know about, and she leaned down to the microphone and said, "Can you hear me?" I said, "Yes," and she said, "I crave your body." There were only about five hundred engineers between Peking and New York, and it caused a big stir in the control room. Well, those were the first words from China by satellite that I know of!

When doing a show like *Today*, the pressure really becomes intense to keep doing things that are new and innovative. When you stop to think about it, you are responsible one way or another, whether it's with a script or an ad lib. To say something new and clever, cheerful and bright, ten hours a week at seven in the morning—I don't think many people are cut out to do that. The pressure really becomes intense.

Hugh Downs did it for ten years or whatever. I don't know how he did it. I know he said he loved it, but with all due respect to my old friend—and we've know each other for years—Hugh's been one of the great liars in the history of television.

I think that after three or four years you've said what you want to say and you've done everything you know how to do.

We obviously make mistakes—I remember saying to Gene Shalit as we were in a station break, "I feel like a fool. God, I wish I could think of something clever to say for the next hour." Gene smiled and looked at me and said, "I wish I could think of just anything to say for the next hour."

On March 14, 1974, Frank Blair retired from *Today.*

Frank Blair's last day on the show

Frank Blair:

" **After twenty-three years, I'm retiring. I've been here long enough and I want to move to other areas of communications. And I want to make way for a younger, more energetic newsman—but I'll always remember *Today*. It has been good to me, and hopefully I've been good for *Today*. "**

Lew Wood replaced Frank Blair.

GERRY
DAVIS

THE **TODAY** **GIRL**

The *Today* show and the world of television were not alone in their viewpoints of women. For the most part, the rest of the world didn't think of women as achievers either. Of course, there were Florence Nightingale, Mrs. Gandhi, and Katharine Hepburn. These women were thought of as a rare breed, and in many respects they were. But women of the fifties, the transitional women, were about to make some noise. These women didn't stop to ask, they just went and did.

Barbara Walters:

❦ I don't think I was waving flags for women. I just thought it was too good an opportunity to miss—to turn down—and it was.

It was the only way. I couldn't turn it down. There was that feeling that women couldn't do it, and I could. Truthfully, I do not know how I did it. Five days a week of *Today* and five days of *Not for Women Only.*

You know, they didn't trust women. One of the reasons I left, and I haven't talked about this, was that I didn't have the right to be consulted, and I wanted that right. The individuals on the show had very little power. I wanted the right to be consulted on the pieces I did and to have some say in the pieces I was assigned. At that time they wouldn't give it to me. I was assigned a piece and that was it unless I could go out and get the story myself. I would kill myself to get to the president, to Begin, to Kissinger, to Yassir Arafat. This was the only way I could do a serious interview. Suddenly it was recognized that I was getting more firsts, and slowly they paid more attention to me. It built my reputation, both good and bad. I was called very aggressive—tough. It was the only way.

It never occurred to me that I would ever leave the *Today* show. I would be there for twenty-five years and, in a gray silk dress, I would be presented with a gold watch and I would retire. There were no opportunities ❧ for women, or very few.

Steve Friedman *(executive producer):*

❝ Barbara Walters certainly got her start here. A lot of women who are on TV certainly owe her a lot. They should give her ten percent of their checks. ❞

In August 1975, while Barbara Walters was on vacation, Betty Furness substituted on *Today.* Betty had been on the show in March and in June, so she was familiar with the routine.

Betty Furness:

❝ I had been a friend of Dave Garroway's, so I'd been aware of the *Today* show since the day it went on the air. I always thought it was terrific, and for many years I tried to be one of the girls on the show. Nobody would talk to me. I mean, *literally* wouldn't talk to me. They didn't want me on. They wanted no part of me. Finally, I realized that it was never going to work. This was in the period through the fifties and sixties.

In '74 I came to work for NBC as a local consumer reporter. One day I was standing by the elevator and Stuart Shulberg, whom I knew casually, said to me, "Would you like to substitute for Barbara Walters someday when she's not on?" I thought I'd died and gone to heaven. I had long since given up any thought of appearing on the show. So I said, "Yeah, that'd be just fine." And I did. I substituted a couple of days while she was away, then a couple of weeks she was away. And then I did a few shows even while she was there. I did a few consumer spots—just as they came up—there was no schedule whatsoever. I'd go on every once in a while and do a consumer spot. And then, when NBC announced that Barbara was leaving, they didn't have anybody to sit down in the chair. They called me and said would I like to do it, and I said I thought I could work it out. ❞

In May 1976, Barbara Walters announced that she would be leaving NBC to co-anchor ABC's *Evening News.* She had seen to it that the gates for women were opened. The race to see who would be the new Queen of *Today* had started.

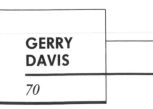

GERRY DAVIS

70

Betty Furness:

❝ For the whole summer before they decided on Jane, I actually did thirteen weeks of the show. I think if you ask that as a trivia question around NBC, if you asked people who jumped in when Barbara left, I don't think you'd get a correct answer. Of course, they had several women who did it a couple days at a time or a week at a time, testing them out. But they'd come in between and then I'd come back the next week till the next one came on. Later, when Paul Friedman was the producer, he said he'd like regular consumer spots. That was the beginning of my doing it on a regular basis, ❞ and I have ever since, for ten years now.

Tom Brokaw:

❝ I think Barbara Walters was maligned in a lot of ways, especially during that important time during Watergate. She gave *Today* a lot of tone, by getting important interviews, and doing them well. Her strengths were not just as "the woman" on the show, but as an aggressive reporter and a journalist with terrific instincts about ❞ what was news and what wasn't.

Jim Hartz and Betty Furness

Beginning in June 1976 *Today* replaced all of its on-camera performers, except Gene Shalit, and most of its executive staff. The executive producer, Paul Friedman, was quick to point out that the cast was not the only aspect of the show that was going to change. The set was going to be redesigned to be more relaxed and comfortable. A new ad-lib approach was going to be attempted to replace detailed scripts. Interviews were to be shortened and emphasis placed on consumer affairs, travel, sports, and health.

There was no question about it that ABC's *Good Morning America,* which celebrated its first anniversary in November 1976, was making *Today* take notice. *Today*'s ratings had begun to slide in late 1974 and, with at least a million viewers having switched the dial, Paul Friedman did not hesitate to concede that "We've been going through a period of great trauma."

Good Morning America had fluff, how-to-cope features, and folkiness all led by its master of ceremonies, David Hartman, and his band of always-smiling cohorts. CBS had its *Morning News.* And *Today* had its problems.

The new set

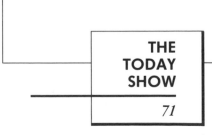

THE
TODAY
SHOW

71

> **Good morning, I'm Tom Brokaw on *Today* with Gene Shalit and Betty Furness and so far so good, I gather.**

That is how Tom Brokaw introduced himself on August 30, 1976, at 7 A.M. to the *Today* show viewers. Yes, indeed, "so far so good," and it became even better.

Tom continued his introduction:

> **It's no real surprise that I will be here each morning at this time with my friends and associates on this program, and I am looking forward to it. We expect to have some fun and we expect, as well, to keep you abreast of what has happened and what is likely to happen in the days to come.**

Tom Brokaw had been NBC's White House correspondent for three years, covering such major events as President Richard Nixon's resignation and Gerald Ford's succession to the presidency. He covered President Ford's visit to Japan and his trip to the People's Republic of China. During the summer of 1976 Brokaw was one of NBC's four floor reporters for TV coverage of the national political conventions.

Tom Brokaw's name had come up before as a possible host for *Today* when Frank McGee died. It was evident then that Tom had outstanding credentials and would be excellent for the job.

Tom Brokaw was and is a reporter. His life-long training as a journalist made him well qualified for *Today*. His soft, deep but firm South Dakotan voice was pleasant for viewers to hear as they woke up and turned on *Today* to learn what was important and interesting in the world. He had poise and wit.

Tom Brokaw:

> **I quickly realized that the show had been allowed to drift before I got there. As a matter of fact, I was very conscious of my role. I had been White House correspondent during a very difficult time in history—Watergate, Gerald Ford—and I came in there with a bulldog mentality, which in retrospect was wrong. My rpm's were driving as fast as they had on the White House lawn.**

Golda Meir and Tom Brokaw

Tom Brokaw was now prime host of *Today* but a hostess still had to be chosen as Betty Furness was only acting as a substitute. Not only was *Today* in a state of flux and change, but for the first time in its twenty-four-year history, active, hard-hitting competition was just a turn of the dial away.

Barbara Walters:

❝ When I was in China the second time and the show was in Chicago, there was a very pretty young girl. She was darling, ❞ and her name was Jane Pauley.

Tom Brokaw:

❝ She's bright and enterprising and engaging and she just happens to be pretty. ❞

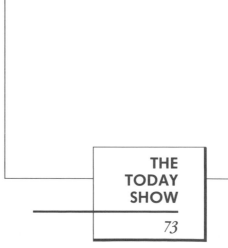

There had been dozens of candidates for Barbara Walters's coveted position. By September 1976, three had reached the finals: Jane Pauley, who had anchored the five o'clock news on NBC's Chicago affiliate; consumer expert Betty Furness, who had substituted for Barbara; and Cassie Mackin, NBC's outstanding Washington correspondent.

On October 11, 1976, Jane Pauley became co-host of *Today*. She had come from Indianapolis to Chicago to New York and was only twenty-five. On her first show, Jane gave a few personal remarks about her experiences before coming to *Today*. Excerpts follow.

Jane Pauley

Jane Pauley:

❛ . . . Maybe you are wondering how I got here. Well, maybe I am, too. I grew up in Indiana, was schooled at Indiana University, and took a degree in political science. I finished a semester early to get out and find what politics really was about. It was a presidential election year. Two weeks before election day, I went to work in a television newsroom and later reported the landslide under which my candidate was buried. It was a timely move. There were no women in that newsroom at the time and the pressure was on to find one. I certainly fit the description. Three years later, NBC came to Indianapolis with a new job offer. I became the first woman to co-anchor a nightly newscast in Chicago. I was twenty-four years old at the time. I'm twenty-five years old now and some people say that's not old enough. I'm inclined to think it makes no difference. But at any rate, there's nothing I can do but anticipate my birthday in two weeks.

In the meantime, Tom and Gene, I expect nothing more on the subject from you except a very nice birthday present. ❜

To which Shalit responded, "In two weeks, you'll be a lot older."

Firmly, succinctly, but with a pretty young smile, Jane Pauley succeeded Barbara Walters. It was obvious to anyone viewing Jane that although she was a bit naïve, with a few rough professional edges to be smoothed, she was a woman who never thought, or perhaps stopped to think, that there would be any doors closed to her. When she came to town, the NBC doors at 30 Rockefeller Plaza were open and the elevator was waiting. There was only one way Jane Pauley was going—and that was up.

• • •

In 1977, *Today* was twenty-five years old with extensive clout, prestige, and heritage.

Tom Brokaw, Jane Pauley, Floyd Kalber, and Gene Shalit, along with contributing guests, made up *Today,* with Paul Friedman as executive producer. It seemed that the viewers found Tom and Jane an agreeable combination, although many found it hard to swallow that now the host and hostess of *Today* were younger than they were. Floyd Kalber's sincere but unconcerned presentation of the news made events seem like they were all under control; panic buttons were unnecessary. Gene Shalit, with his electric shock look, and who had been on the show longer than any of his cohorts, was just Gene.

Twenty-fifth anniversary

LIVE FROM LONDON

On June 7, 1977, *Today* presented a special edition lasting more than five hours from London of Elizabeth II's Silver Jubilee as Queen and head of the British Commonwealth.

Coverage began at 5 A.M. New York time and ratings showed that *Today* audiences did not mind getting up before dawn in order to be "part of" the Jubilee.

Of course, this was not the first time *Today* had been to London. *Today* had done a remote show from London in the fifties, but this time was going to be different. Now, with technological advances, viewers were going to be able to be there simultaneously, as the events took place.

As Tom Brokaw presided over the coverage from a London TV studio, *Today* viewers saw the beginning of the royal procession from Buckingham Palace to Saint Paul's Cathedral. They saw the Queen emerge from the palace in a golden stagecoach with Prince Phillip at her side and Prince Charles on a horse behind them. The service at Saint Paul's lasted almost an hour and was covered in full. After the service, viewers saw the Queen, accompanied by Prince Phillip, talking to and greeting her subjects and foreign guests. As viewers were finishing their breakfast—8:37 A.M. New York time—they saw the Queen enter Guildhall for lunch with prime ministers and foreign ministers of British Commonwealth countries. No cameras had been permitted in Guildhall.

There were other features presented on the more "normal" London life by the NBC News correspondent based in London, Paul Cunningham.

Jane Pauley reported from the Princess Louise, a pub, where she interviewed some of the Queen's subjects. A young man told Pauley, "It's a nice thing to have a queen," to which a young woman responded, "Supporting the Queen is a waste of money. I think Prince Charles, if he were a man at all, would say he doesn't want to be King."

Anthony Howard, editor of *The New Statesman* magazine, told Tom Brokaw how he wanted to see the monarchy "phased out" and he thought the royal family costly. He conceded that as a symbol the Queen is "good for exports and tourists" but, "Why doesn't she open Buckingham Palace to the public as the White House is open?"

A few minutes before the Queen began her short speech, the

GERRY
DAVIS

cameras were back at Guildhall, and at 10:07 A.M. the *Today* coverage was concluded.

For many viewers the *Today* show was a morning rock on which to lean, which one reached for before starting the day. And for another group, watching *Today* afforded the reason not to have to talk in the morning. And of course there was the other group that would say, "Why do you have to say or listen to anyone or anything in the morning? Can't you just wake up and enjoy the day's beginning?"

On January 8, 1979, a new *Today* theme composed by Ray Ellis that incorporated the notes of the NBC chimes—bing bong bing (notes G, E, C)—was heard by the viewers. The theme was recorded by a twenty-one piece orchestra and was used at the opening of the program, during the breaks, and at the close of each day's telecast. The chimes, a symbol of NBC since 1927, had a broader historical distinction. They were the first purely audible "service mark" ever registered by the U.S. Patent Office.

Visually, there were also other changes. A new set that featured a panoramic photograph of Manhattan as a backdrop was created to add, as producer Paul Friedman said, "a comfortable area for conversation."

Along with hosts Tom Brokaw and Jane Pauley, Floyd Kalber was on hand to report news and sports. Bob Ryan gave the weather forecast.

Gene Shalit's participation in the show was expanded. Haynes Johnson of the *Washington Post,* Ellen Goodman and Mike Barnicle of *The Boston Globe,* syndicated columnist George F. Will, and, as a political commentator, Georgia State Senator Julian Bond were all now contributors to *Today.*

"Cross Country" reports were also offered by correspondents Jack Perkins and Eric Burns. Dick Schaap's segments presented the "Sportsman-of-the-Week." "What's Up" was a feature presenting new trends and ideas; there was also a segment devoted to entertainment.

In April, Joe Bartelme replaced Paul Friedman as executive producer, and in May 1979, Steve Friedman, no relation to Paul Friedman, was named producer.

Today certainly had enough participants, but did they have enough viewers?

COMPETITION

Joe Bartelme announced that changes again were to be made, and they began to take place at a rapid rate. New sets, new formats, and more new faces. Jane, Tom, and Gene were in charge of worldly matters. Former fashion model Alanna Davis was added to do segments of light news features and human-interest stories. Phil Donahue was also added and presented an abbreviated version of his hour show.

For years *Today* had never had any real competition and, without it, *Today* could do almost whatever it wanted to do.

Tom Brokaw:

❛ I remember we put on a famous harpsichordist in a long gold brocade dress. She played for fifteen minutes. I knew it was a mistake. I realized we couldn't do that anymore. That time had come to an end. You could do segments [of that length] in the old days when there were no other morning shows. Now we had two competitors. ❜

It was a case of monkey see, monkey do. In 1975, when *Good Morning America* first started, their solution was to be more like *Today* than *Today*. *Good Morning America* seemed to adhere to the original Pat Weaver memo on the subject of his idea for morning TV, which said:

> We want America to shave, to eat, to dress, to get to work on time. But we also want America to be well informed, to be amused, to be lightened in spirit and in heart, and to be reinforced in inner resolution through knowledge. Seven to nine A.M. will be the Sun Valley, Palm Springs, and Miami Beach of TV.

Today was suffering a mid-life crisis. *Good Morning America* was suffering growing pains. CBS's *Morning Show* was just suffering.

At CBS in 1979, they were trying very hard. Charles Kuralt, the wonderful soothing laureate of the common man, was made the *Morning Show* anchorman and ratings increased, although it was still only a one-hour show.

Morning TV audiences had increased almost 29 percent and, more significantly, began to talk about what they had seen on the shows. Only a certain group had once confessed to watching TV before evening. Formerly it had been like saying you had a Bloody Mary or a glass of wine at lunch. But intelligent reporting, interesting sequents, and timely coverage could indeed take place before evening, so people were talking about it.

Critics were also sharpening their pencils. They were going to have a heyday filling columns with their words on the battles, the knock-down drag-outs, of the morning shows. They would dissect, analyze, scrutinize, and possibly fantasize about what they were *really* watching between seven and nine A.M.

Marvin Kitman (*writing in* The New Leader*):*

❧ To me Brokaw is not a very warm person to wake up to. His personality is cold, and his face has the tightness of a man on a perpetual diet. Nor does it help that Brokaw's principal sidekick, Jane Pauley, whose major journalistic qualification is that she looks like a younger Barbara Walters, can't interview, write, or think like Barbara. After almost two years on the job, Jane still appears puzzled by the whole affair, incapable of doing anything without that electric plug in her ear barking important instructions from the control room—"Open your mouth," "Raise your hand," "Turn left." ❧

At the offices of *Today*, panic was nesting.

Philip Terzian (*writing in* Commonweal*):*

❧ I have never been able to look at *Good Morning America* for more than a few minutes. It is so excruciatingly amiable and simple-minded that I find myself embarrassed on its behalf. Its master of ceremonies, David Hartman, moves back and forth easily between Salt II and Rona Barrett, and doesn't notice the difference. ❧

In spite of Satchel Paige's advice, "Don't look back, someone might be gaining on you," *Today* and NBC officials did look back and, yes, someone was gaining on them.

In January 1980, *Today*'s domination of the morning airwaves was finally broken, despite the critics, by ABC's *Good Morning America.* From January to August, ABC was either even with NBC or it was tops in the Nielsen ratings. Because viewers tend to leave the dial where it was when they went to bed, during *Shōgun* and the World Series NBC inched ahead. During the months of October and November, *Today* and *GMA* bounced back and forth for first place.

NBC executives were taking long looks at their competition and wondering how and who they could find to come up with a winning formula. As tall, low-keyed, relaxed, and sincere seemed to be the ingredients for a male host, NBC looked for just that.

For the female hostess, bright-eyed, smiling, and wholesome were the prerequisites. When Jane Pauley was on her honeymoon with Garry Trudeau in June 1980, Mariette Hartley was brought in to substitute. Still the soufflé did not rise. The temperature and environment were not right. The mix of Jane, Tom, and Gene was missing something. Their basic ingredients were of superior quality but a catalyst was needed. Then, all of the ABC morning ingredients—tall, low-keyed, relaxed, sincere, bright-eyed, smiling, and wholesome—were found all rolled up in one person. Enter Mr. Willard Scott, March 10, 1980.

GERRY
DAVIS

WILLARD

For thirteen years, Willard Scott had been the weatherman at NBC's Washington affiliate. Willard had his own distinctive style, but what was easily understood on a local level needed a bit of getting used to for national television audiences. Was he using his hash browns, moonshine, love thy neighbor, hearty ha-ha, and good-ole-boy talk as just an act, or did he really mean what he said?

Audiences do not like to be duped, especially early in the morning. And when they don't understand they tend to complain. Initially, complaints did come in, but before long people realized that Willard was for real—he wasn't acting.

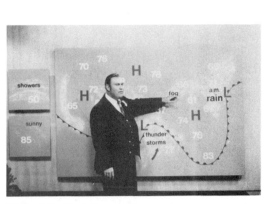

Willard Scott at the weather map

Willard Scott:

❝ **My plan was to fill the void left by J. Fred Muggs. If you watch, you'll see that I'm trying to weave a web of love. I want to make the whole country feel as if we are one. I may be a cornball, but I am me—not a sophisticated, slick, New York wazoo act.** ❞

By the end of 1980, there were no credibility gaps in Willard's performance. He was receiving approximately two thousand fan letters a week.

Mr. Willard Scott is just Willard no matter where he is. What you see is *not* what you get when you meet Willard. What you get is better than what you see, and what you see is mighty darn good. No frills, no jabs, no beating around the bush. No fake smiles, no broken promises, no pretensions. Friendly teasing, now and then, to Mr. Friedman or an NBC executive. But nothing malicious or even inaccurate. Overweight, balding, with a heart even too big for his oversized frame, that's Willard Scott.

Morrison Krus (assistant to Willard Scott):

❝ **Willard had purchased a very expensive suit that he had always wanted. Ironically, the day the**

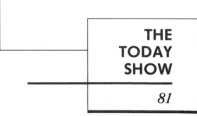

Willard Scott as Carmen Miranda

suit was delivered to his office he received a letter from an elderly lady saying that she and her husband would go to church regularly, but that her husband did not have a suit to wear. When Willard saw the letter, he had me make the necessary phone calls and send the suit to the woman. **,**

For Willard there is only one way to do something, and that is 100 percent. Willard would like to have a show of his own and most probably will as soon as he decides the format, but that does not mean he will leave *Today.*

Steve Friedman:

(Scott is as important to *Today* as Brando was to *The Godfather*. He may not be in every scene, but his presence pervades the show. ,

Willard could never be accused of being one of TV's all too many pretty, plastic boys. Husband, father of two grown daughters, gentleman, farmer, ex-radio personality, religious, the first Ronald McDonald and more, that's Willard Scott.

Don Haynie (unit manager):

(Just being with Willard is a guarantee to have a wonderful time. He loves being with people. Good, simple, straight, unpretentious, real people. ,

Willard travels thousands of miles a year, appearing at openings, fairs, festivals, parades, balls, and celebrations. He is an unmatched public relations force for NBC.

Weather and Willard are synonymous. As he stands in front of the weather map stating the weather conditions across the country and warning of hazardous situations, he makes it seem as if everything will be all right.

Hundreds of items are sent to Willard each year with hopes he will show them on the air. Fruits, baked goods, handicrafts, vegetables, sporting goods, flowers, animals, fish, you name it, Willard has probably received it.

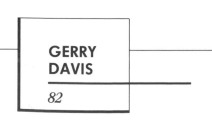

GERRY
DAVIS

Eric Chasanoff *(meteorologist)*:

❝ One day a box arrived for Willard. A temporary secretary was helping that day in the office, opening and labeling items that had arrived. Suddenly a piercing scream was heard. We rushed to see what was the matter. In the middle of the floor, with the temporary as far away as possible, we see an open box ❞ with *live* black wiggly eels.

Joe Witte *(substitute weatherman for Scott)*:

❝ People often ask me if Willard is really the way he appears on the air. He is even more fun in person. If you go somewhere to dinner with him, you find out he is known everywhere. You can't walk down the street without someone saying hi. Of course, Willard takes time to return ❞ the greetings and chats a bit with them.

Willard Scott as Boy George

In the Washington, D.C., area where people have listened to Willard for years on the radio, they refer to him as *their* Willard, but thanks to *Today,* Willard has become *our* Willard. As Larry King wrote in his *U.S.A. Today* column, "Willard Scott should be declared a national treasure."

When Willard was asked how he would like to be remembered he said, "As a real person." Asked if he had any helpful hints about life, he replied, "Love people—it comes back."

Nothing can be taken for granted, particularly in the business of live morning television.

Tom Brokaw:

❝ We were at the Strategic Air Command and doing this opening. I was tucked back in a little recessed panel in the control room, and the idea was to shoot the opening looking down a long control panel of the SAC, deep down underground in Omaha. There were lights in this recessed area that I was tucked inside, and I was getting real warm in there. I had to be in there a few minutes before I

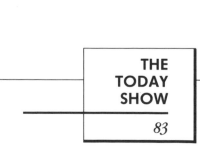

stepped out and said, "Good morning, I'm Tom Brokaw," and God, I thought, am I getting warm. Then they were saying, "Three, two, one," and I looked down and my blazer had caught fire on my shoulder. I stepped out, slapping my shoulder, trying to put the flames out, saying, "Good morning." I did the rest of the program with my 💬 **sleeve, which had come off, taped on.**

Since the days of *Today*'s first producers, Richard Pinkham and Mort Werner, there have been many producers of the *Today* show. In May 1980, Steve Friedman took the reins of *Today* and became executive producer.

Steve Friedman:

💬 **TV shows die from within when people start taking the audience for granted.** 💬

What did the new executive producer have to work with? Jane and Tom were still at the helm, but instead of seeming "pompous and puzzled" as they did in 1977, the *Today* hosts were a more friendly Tom and a more relaxed but fastidious Jane. They had become full-grown professionals in their trade. Both were very good. Gene Shalit would articulate in his own fashion from the Critics Corner. Richard Valeriani was the Washington correspondent; Dr. Art Ulene kept audiences informed of medical happenings, and there was a large roster of contributors on other topics, such as Betty Furness with her consumer reports and Bryant Gumbel on sports. And finally there was the largest asset of all, Willard Scott.

The new executive producer had a plan to speed up the show. Instead of an old-fashioned fox trot, he was guiding *Today* into an electric boogie. Technology had come a long way since 1952, and Steve Friedman was going to put it to use on *Today*. Prominent guests were not going to have to come to New York to be part of the show, instead *Today* was going to go to them whenever possible. *Today* specialists, particularly Richard Valeriani and Bryant Gumbel, were going to have their assignments expanded. The news would become more humanized by their insights.

Everyone had ideas about the causes of the *Today* problems as well as the cures. Some said the lowered ratings were due to the anchors. Some thought it was the lack of stability and continual changes on the network executive level. Or it was too much seriousness. Too little fluff. Not enough entertainment. Not enough comaraderie. Too much, too little, whatever, Steve Friedman was in charge, and his goal was to see *Today* number one.

Tom Brokaw:

❻ **The crown jewel of my tenure on *Today* was the Royal Wedding. It was a wonderful, exciting time, perfectly suited for what we do. I am not a great admirer of royalty. I have nothing against Charles and Diana, just the institution of royalty. But I must admit I got there and I got swept up in the majesty, the royalty, the romance of these two people.**

You could not be cynical about it because it meant so much to so many. I have friends who live in cabins out in Wyoming, and they got up at two A.M. ❾ to get into Jackson Hole to watch the show.

Correspondents Tom Brokaw, Jane Pauley, and John Chancellor covered the Royal Wedding. Also in London were Willard Scott, Jim Bitterman, and Eric Burns conducting interviews from various locations. In spite of the political and economic turmoil Great Britain was then going through, the fairy-tale scenario and pageantry of the Royal Wedding was an event made for television. Prince Charles had said at a dinner for American correspondents, "We British do this rather well [pageantry] . . . my fiancée and I intend to give them a real show."

Today's coverage of the Royal Wedding was excellent and ratings were good, but once the splendid pomp was over, it was back to more regular happenings. The competition among the three morning shows continued.

In the fall of 1981, NBC announced that Tom Brokaw would be leaving the *Today* show to assume a new assignment as an anchorman on the *NBC Nightly News.*

In his final appearance as *Today* host, on December 18, 1981, Tom Brokaw conducted a live interview with President Ronald Reagan. The interview was conducted via two-way audiovideo hookup with the president in the White House and Tom Brokaw in New York.

Tom Brokaw:

❻ **There are no other two-hour programs to deal with the news except the morning shows. And**

Jane Pauley and Willard Scott in London

there is no subject that is inappropriate to the *To-day* show. Therefore, if your interests are wide ranging, you could indulge yourself in any of those and from a purely selfish point of view. It was a very instructive, broadening experience for me. I learned a lot, and I like to think that people watching learned a lot, too. I made friends, I learned about new subjects, and was able to go to exotic places. "

GERRY DAVIS

COMPETITION CONTINUES

There is intense competition among the morning shows to book newsmaking guests and celebrities. There is nothing genteel or polite about it. "Guest-grabbers," as they are called, frequently incorporate a mixture of Sherlock Holmes, Houdini, the CIA, female intuition, alacrity, and *chutzpah* to get a guest first. Guests are often "hidden" in an unsuspecting hotel. Disguises are used. Guest-sitting is the norm—that is, someone from the show stays with the guest to be sure the competition does not "steal" him or her. Protocol, honesty, gamesmanship, and sportsmanship are all pushed aside, when it comes to obtaining a guest *first*!

Good Morning America often will pay a guest to appear on their show. NBC and CBS pay in goods and services—first-class tickets, hotel rooms, limousines, flowers, and champagne.

Guests sometimes request that if they appear on a morning show certain topics must be avoided. Often one show will agree to the request while the other two will not. Some sought-after guests simply refuse to appear. Other guests, in order to placate the three morning shows, will tape three different interviews to be aired simultaneously. A thirty-second lead airing it can mean "a first."

Janice "J.J." DeRosa (researcher and *former assistant to the executive producer*):

❝ We literally stake out a place. In order to get the Jarvik 7 heart man we staked out the hotel day and night. All we had to go by was an A.P. photo. Anybody that looked like him we would go up to. ❞

In December 1983, Navy flier Lt. Robert L. Goodman, Jr.'s plane was shot down over the Syrian-controlled portion of Lebanon during a United States raid. The Reverend Jesse Jackson helped negotiate his release. *Today* established the first communication, January 3, 1984, between Goodman and his mother following his release. It was an emotional ten-minute conversation. Later in the week, *Today* obtained another first related to the incident.

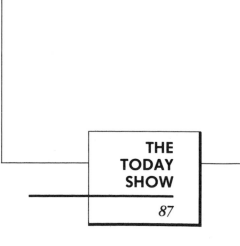

Cheryl Wells *(researcher):*

❝ One of our researchers had become very friendly with Officer Goodman's wife and had booked her on the show. We were the first ones to get her. On the scheduled morning our researcher went to pick her up in the limo. Arriving a few minutes early, she found a limo from the major competition. Mrs. Goodman had been told they were from NBC! People can be very unprincipled.

One of the functions of a researcher is to try to book guests first. You are always in fear that the competition is going to get the guest before you. When a big news story breaks, you know everyone in the world is going after these people.

When the TWA plane was hijacked [in June 1985], we had to reach the families of the people on the plane. You have to handle it in a very delicate way because these families don't know what's happening to their loved ones.

We had a passenger list. The other networks had a passenger list. We were all calling. The NBC News executives decided that *Today* would invite three families to go to Frankfurt, since that was where the hijacked passengers and crew were to be released. One of the people I had been talking to was Jill Brown, wife of hostage Robert Brown. She accepted the invitation to go to Frankfurt. Then we got two other families. I took them to the plane. There was press on the plane already and more when we got to Frankfurt. They were all crowding around us. It was most unpleasant. We had to walk through some girl's camera shot so she took her mike and hit me in the face. She went crazy in front of the guest. It was embarrassing, but I stood there and said, "Don't you ever do that to me again." All the press was following us. It was a zoo. ❞

Another Researcher:

❝ It is really hard at times, like when we had to go and talk to the families of the [*Challenger*] astronauts who were killed. You really don't want to, but then if we don't get to them, *GMA* will. ❞

GERRY
DAVIS

88

Cheryl Wells:

❝ We were at the 1986 Super Bowl. The "Refrigerator" [William Perry] and his wife were scheduled to be on *Today* first, and I had become very friendly with his wife. In fact, she was planning to take behind-the-scenes pictures of the Super Bowl and then bring them on the show. The night before they were to be on, I found that the Refrigerator was not at his hotel but was staying with his wife at her hotel. The next morning I got a call from Phil Grossman, a *Today* writer, saying that the other network was trying to get to the Fridge because they wanted to tape something with him before he went on *Today*. Phil said I should try to stall them until just before they were to go. I got the Fridge and his wife out of the hotel, into the car, and I said, "So, Fridge, are you hungry?" He said yes, so I took them out to eat, and we got to the set five minutes before they were going on the air. The other network was furious. As far as I was con- ❞ cerned, they could tape after.

In November 1981, it was announced that Bryant Gumbel would become co-anchor of *Today* with Jane Pauley, assuming his responsibilities on January 4, 1982. Bryant was a familiar face to *Today* audiences. Since 1980, he had been giving thrice-weekly sports reports.

Steve Friedman:

❝ Bryant is one of the best broadcasters I've ever come across. Sports fans admire his work and even those people who are not avid sports fans enjoy his cool, calm, and ❞ thoughtful presentations.

Bryant began his broadcasting career in 1972 as weekend sportscaster for KNBC Los Angeles. By 1976, he had been appointed the station's sports director. In 1975, he was co-host for NBC Sports' NFL pregame show.

Now *Today* was gambling on Gumbel.

Bryant Gumbel (*in* Glamour *magazine*):

❝ I obviously think it's going to work, otherwise I wouldn't be here. ❞

Nielsen rating points were being watched like a speck on a radar-scope. Three tenths of a point or seven tenths of a point sound like minuscule amounts, and they are, if you are looking at tenths on a ruler. But not so on the Nielsen rating; when *GMA* held a three tenths of a ratings point edge, they were able to charge $2,000 more a commercial minute. Tenths of a point can mean millions of dollars in annul revenues for the networks.

Could it be done? Would it be done? Jane Pauley, Bryant Gumbel, Chris Wallace, Willard Scott, Gene Shalit, and the entire

Chris Wallace, Gene Shalit, Jane Pauley, Willard Scott, Bryant Gumbel

Today staff were giving it their all to fight for the number-one morning spot.

Chris Wallace became Washington anchor of *Today* in January 1982. A native of Chicago, graduate of Harvard, national reporter for *The Boston Globe,* political commentator on WGBH-Boston, Wallace joined NBC as a reporter with WNBC-TV in New York in 1975. In 1980, he was a reporter at the national conventions. Since 1981, a Washington correspondent for special reports on the *NBC Nightly News,* Chris Wallace joined the *Today* staff with an outstanding knowledge of national politics.

In June of 1982, Wallace and Bryant Gumbel provided live and taped coverage of Ronald Reagan's first European trip as president. Reports were filed by Wallace on the first formal meeting between Presidents Francois Mitterand and Reagan. He also interviewed Treasury secretary Donald Regan, who was traveling with the presidential party. Highlights of the meeting between the president and Pope John Paul II were also presented, as was coverage of the London visit by the president—his speech to Parliament and his horseback ride with Queen Elizabeth II. Completing the European trip, Gumbel and Wallace conducted extensive reports from Bonn.

Steve Friedman:

❝ With this kind of team we could win. We were the new kids on the block then. GMA was a very successful show, but let me tell you, Gumbel, Pauley, Shalit, Scott, and Wallace ❞ were going to be hard to beat.

What did Bryant Gumbel have to say in 1982 about Bryant Gumbel? As quoted in *Glamour,* he thought he was "cute rather than handsome, nice rather than sexy, friendly rather than suave."

Steve Friedman:

❝ I've always known that Bryant could be the biggest star of television news and information. He's the quickest person I've ever met. You tell him something in his ear on an IFB [earphone] and one second later it's done. He's ❞ gentle, pleasant, but tough.

Bryant was not the first to switch from the world of sports to morning news. There had been Joe Garagiola before him on To-

day, from 1967 to 1973. Nor would Bryant be the first black to anchor a network news show. There was Ed Bradley at CBS and Max Robinson at ABC.

Although since joining the show in October 1976 she had never been limited to working in the studio, Jane Pauley's responsibilities were now increased. Willard was becoming a topic of conversation, and Gene Shalit was expanding his critiques.

The cast was beginning to get to know one another, work well together, and they seemed to enjoy it. The ambiance of the *Today* show was definitely changing for the better, but there were those whose caustic comments were still appearing in print.

McHugh and Hoffman (*Washington media consulting firm*):

❝ **Gumbel is a really smart-assy young kid and co-host Jane Pauley is vacuous. They're not strong enough to compete with GMA's entertainment style or to play the hard-news game with CBS's Morning News. Today will get squeezed from both sides.** ❞

Michael Wexler (*New York advertising executive*):

❝ **The Today show is tired, and people are tired of the Today show.** ❞

NBC had a rating loss. CBS *Morning News,* now anchored by Bill Kurtis and Diane Sawyer, had gained in ratings. *Good Morning America* was number one and, due to their lofty ratings, was now able to charge $12,000 for a thirty-second commercial.

In *Newsweek, GMA*'s associate producer, John Goodman, stated why TV's breakfast king should enjoy a long reign:

David Hartman has been on more years than anyone on NBC and CBS, and the viewers feel comfortable with him. And our longevity gives us a lot of advantages in booking guests. Menachem Begin knows who David Hartman is. I'm not sure if he knows Bryant Gumbel.

Steve Friedman:
❝ **We're not panicking.** ❞

In 1982, Ronald Reagan was president and George Bush was vice-president. A loaf of bread was 65¢, a gallon of milk was $2.19 and a pound of butter was $1.48. The average annual income was $21,073. A new Ford car was $7,983 and a gallon of gas was $1.22. The St. Louis Cardinals beat the Milwaukee Brewers for the World Series, and the speed at the Indy was 162.026 mph. The Dow Jones Index was 1,094.50. An ounce of gold was $350, silver $7.31, and copper 77¢. Meryl Streep and Ben Kingsley were box-office attractions and the song "Rosanna" was on top of the hits.

In 1952, the *Today* show was the only morning television show. In 1982, there were three major television channels, not to mention numerous other channels airing something.

The Thirtieth Anniversary Show was just a day away. Plans for an on-air celebration had been in the works for weeks. But then:

```
        STOP!    NEWS BREAK!

AIR FLORIDA BOEING 737 JET HITS WASHINGTON, D.C.'S 14TH
STREET BRIDGE. 78 DIE, INCLUDING PASSENGERS AND PEOPLE
ON THE BRIDGE.
```

Although the news was against it, the celebration went on the next day as planned.

THE THIRTIETH ANNIVERSARY SHOW

It is difficult to describe what the thirtieth anniversary—Thursday, January 14, 1982—was like at *Today*. The assemblage of past hosts, co-hosts, and show personalities was formidable and impressive, and whether you were at the show or watching, you could not help but share in the euphoric feeling of being part of the longest-running morning television show.

Steve Friedman:

❝ It was history! It was history! Everyone we wanted came. ❞

Thirtieth anniversary

Dave Garroway, the Communicator, was there. The original host still displayed his unequaled grace, style, and salesmanship. Along with Jane, Bryant, and Gene, sat Tom Brokaw, John Chancellor, Hugh Downs, Barbara Walters, Jack Lescoulie, Frank Blair, and the originator of *Today*, Sylvester "Pat" Weaver. Also present were Betty Furness, Estelle Parsons, Lee Meriwether, Betsy Palmer, Joe Garagiola, Jim Hartz, Ed Newman, Florence Henderson, and Helen O'Connell. These were the people you saw, but equally important to this gathering were the behind-the-scenes people—the studio crews, the control room staff, and the office staff.

It was a wonderful reunion. Barbara Walters recalled what it was like to be a woman in the early days of television and how women were thought of as decorative twinklers. There was a tribute to the late Frank McGee. It was a very nostalgic morning. As the big hand neared "straight up," Garroway's theme song "Sentimental Journey" was heard and the old master communicator raised his right hand and gave, for the last time, his trademark sign off: "Peace."

Steve Friedman:

❝ When Garroway did "Peace," a lot of people in the studio broke up. ❞

July 21, 1982, six months later, Dave Garroway took his life.

Frank Blair:

❝ He once said to me, "That television camera is my best friend." He started the whole school of communicating. He had the ability to communicate one-to-one through the camera. ❞

Jack Lescoulie:

❝ He was an original. He was one of a kind. There won't be another one like him. His whole attitude was to make the show go and he believed, from the very first minute on the air, that it would go. ❞

PEACE

The morning show battle for first place continued. The audiences were out there, the trick was to get them to watch the show, and

of course each network considered its show *the* show. "Tricks" were tried continually. Change the sets. Extend the interviews. Add more segments. Be more glamorous. Lighten up. Do more outside the studio. Amuse, shock, sympathize, dramatize, expose—everything and anything. Perhaps the answer was to have one six-hour morning show with *everyone* from all the morning shows participating!

Larry Grossman:

In 1983, when I returned to NBC as president of NBC News, I went around and talked to the affiliates. On everyone's priority list was to do something about the *Today* show, which was in danger of falling into third place. I spent a lot of time talking to people, getting advice, going to the program every morning. Everything was in question. The show, the producers, Bryant, Jane. Gene Shalit probably wasn't liked around the rest of the country. Willard did weather but couldn't do anything else. Major changes had to be made.

The ingredients were there. Sets had been changed repeatedly and formats revamped. Each person was doing his or her job. The ingredients were good. Nothing was sour. But still it was not mixing.

During interviews questions were being asked, but the answers were ignored. The next question was being composed before the previous one was completed. There was a lot of interrupting and spots were too short. Something had to be done.

Larry Grossman:

We did what we could to slow the show down and to make our people feel confident and comfortable. Somehow they [the on-camera staff] had to develop that team spirit.

On this modern high-tech planet we live on, there are three sure winners: the American flag, apple pie, and motherhood. *Today* could have two out of three—the American flag is flown outside the NBC studios and *Today*'s budget could certainly have a line for apple pie, but motherhood, the all-time winner, could prove a problem, even for NBC.

In the spring of 1983, Jane Pauley supplied the missing element. She was pregnant!

One should not overlook that motherhood had already been a part of *GMA* with Joan Lundon's pregnancies but, for some reason, Jane's pregnancy was different. Perhaps it was because she was expecting twins.

Jane's pregnancy was carefully watched, and as it progressed so did the stacks of mail with wishes and advice. Thoughtful gifts poured in, too.

In November, Jimmy Stewart was on the show. Admitting to his reputation for occasional absentmindedness, and also as a father of twin girls, he told Jane this story:

Jimmy Stewart:

It's a wonderful idea, twins. I think if they could invent things so you don't have *any*, I don't see why you can't invent something so you can have two at a time. They're never alone. They always have each other. After the twins were born, Gloria [his wife] was quite ill for a while. I'd visit her every day at the hospital. The day arrived when she was going to come home. I went down and parked the car in the parking lot and went up the elevator and checked with her. She was all dressed, and I said, "Fine, I'll go down and get the car and meet you at the patients' entrance." So I went down and got in my car and started home. Gloria got down to the entrance and the nurse said "Well, where is he?" And Gloria said, "Don't worry. He went home. He forgot. Let's go back upstairs and call him."

Well, we've been married thirty-five years, and I suppose it will take another thirty-five to get clear of that one.

Connie Chung, multi-award winning correspondent, anchor of NBC *News at Sunrise,* was named to substitute for Jane Pauley when she left for her three-month maternity leave.

On December 30, 1983, Rachel and Ross Trudeau were born!

John Palmer, a twenty-two-year veteran of NBC News joined the *Today* show in September 1983. Prior to joining the show he was White House correspondent for NBC for three years and in the late seventies, he was based at the NBC News bureau in Paris. He was the first broadcast journalist to receive the Merriman Fund Award for Excellence in Presidential News coverage.

Jane Pauley and Connie Chung

A native of Kingsport, Tennessee, whose first paying job after high school was that of a radio announcer at $1 an hour, he admits that he thoroughly enjoys his work but wishes that interviews could be longer. "Just when an interview is getting interesting—time is up!"

John Palmer:

❝ *Today* is well suited to me because I am the father of two little girls. I usually get home for a late lunch with them, take naps at the same time, and go to bed at night when they do. Unlike most fathers, I see a lot of ❞ the kids during the week.

In 1984, John was grand marshal for the July 4th Parade in Kingsport, and *Today* covered it. It was a special event in his record book. Also special, in another sense, was the morning he began the news and, thinking it was just a rehearsal, said, "Good Morning. Howdy, Jane," and stopped talking!

John is firm but easygoing, with a streak of humor that is much in evidence when he sits in for Bryant.

In real life one learns that moving—changing one's four walls—does not remove internal or personal problems, but in the television world of *Today* that theory was proved incorrect. In 1984, those at NBC who decide such things announced that *Today* would start moving around on a grand scale—doing remotes.

John Palmer

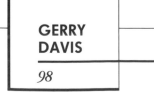

GERRY
DAVIS

REMOTES

Because there are entertainment aspects of *Today* as well as news, the job of planning a remote is awesome. When a large remote is in the planning stages, a survey is done. For a survey a unit manager, a producer, a director, and a technical director will go to the site or sites and plan what is going to be done and then how to do it. The remote often starts six to seven months ahead of the broadcast date. Unit managers schedule people, and they schedule machinery—videotape equipment, cameras, studios, satellite time—whatever is needed.

To produce a remote myriad details must be considered and decided and alternatives planned. Where will the home base be during the remote? Are the telecasting facilities adequate? Areas must be defined and prepared—lighting, cameras, microphones, props, transportation, accommodations, makeup, wardrobe, coordination of crews, security, typewriters, phones, office supplies, medical facilities, runners—and translators, if there is a language difference.

More often than not special permission must be obtained to originate from a desired place, be it a street site, a museum, a hotel, or a selected state or country. A show cannot just arrive and begin to televise.

A week-long *Today* show remote will have ten hours or less of actual air time, but the hours of preparation will be hundreds of times that. The costs are huge, but the rewards in staff pride and ratings make it worthwhile.

There are six unit managers, headed by the production manager, on the *Today* staff. The unit manager's job is vital.

Jeff Hark (production manager):

❝ We are the glue that holds the show together. The producers, writers, and directors decide what they want to do, and it is up to us to make it happen. All sorts of facilities have to be ordered, and they can range from the sublime to the ridiculous. Like, "Jeff, hi! I need three hours of edit time to put together a piece." Or, "Jeff, hi! We're taking the show to South America next year."

Unit managers travel a lot and do some very bi-

Unit managers: Mike Castro, Don Haynie, Liz Shannon, Chris Florez, David Naggiar, Jeff Hark, Susan Sullivan

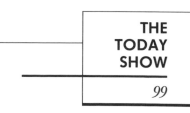

zarre things. Looking for locations, they see more roofs, basements, cellars, back alleys, and strange places than probably anyone else on the staff.

Unit managers do not work for the executive producer of *Today*, but for the vice-president of finance for the news division.

The unit managers keep track of how much it all costs and also exercise some control over how much it costs. We are supposed to be the watch-dogs of the budget of the *Today* show. **9**

Liz Shannon (unit manager):

6 It's a complicated process, and it takes weeks and weeks, with varying degrees of difficulty, depending on where you are and how cooperative the people are around you. You just start and you deal with the day-to-day problems of setting up offices, running the office, paying people—and getting the job done.

In many places NBC has a bureau, and if you have a bureau it makes things much easier. The bureau can make the necessary contacts. If not, you deal with outside production companies. And that can be scary because you are **9** relying on their reputations.

Don Haynie:

6 On the big remotes, where almost everyone goes along, there is a tremendous amount of work. When we are in a strange city, we are often asked to find things like chairs that have to be a certain height with high backs. Usually we are asked to find this item at a weird hour. We usually find them—maybe not in the exact color—but we find them. **9**

Jeff Hark:

6 Unit managers become the mommies and daddies of the unit. They come to us for everything that anybody needs. People get sick, we take care of that. People need **9** things, they come to us.

Don Haynie:

❝ When you go on a remote, as soon as you get off the plane you start working. Sometimes you get off the plane at one A.M. and you are up at three A.M. Many times I've gone into a hotel and it is after midnight and I ask for a three o'clock wake-up call and I'm asked, "Three P.M.?" "No, three A.M.!" ❞

Janice "J.J." DeRosa:

❝ On remotes we really work. We sometimes have language barriers, know nothing about a place, and are building from scratch. Sometimes we are working through interpreters. The only thing we really get to do is to go to dinner. It is not until the show is on the air that things start to calm down. ❞

Don Haynie:

❝ A unit manager has to be firm but courteous. You have to please a lot of people. You take the credit and you take the blame. You have to get twenty-five people across the street on one subway token, and everyone wants to go first class. ❞

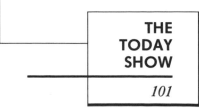

LIVE FROM MOSCOW

On September 6, 1984, a major step for *Today* in the ratings race was made. Indeed, one might say it was a major step in television history. *Today* was going to telecast live from Moscow. Bryant Gumbel was there to do a week of reports from inside the Soviet Union. There were many difficulties inherent in interviewing Soviet public officials, and Bryant offered an explanation from Moscow to the *Today* viewers.

Bryant Gumbel in Moscow

Bryant Gumbel:

❝ There is such a striking difference between where you are and where I sit. Interviews are relatively unheard of here. Here a statement is drafted by committee and, once read, examination or clarification, well, that's thought to be unnecessary. Beyond that, the competitive nature of political life here makes it hazardous, relatively, for one official to step forward, apart from his committee, to be either praised or blamed personally for what was a committee's decision. People interviewed in the states are thought to be in the limelight. Here they are perceived to be under a microscope. That is discomforting indeed. ❞

Soviet Deputy Minister of Foreign Trade Aleksy Manzhulo; cosmonaut Svetlana Savitskaya; Tatiana Yankelevich and Alexei Semonov, stepchildren of Soviet dissident Andrei Sakharov; Soviet Central Committee member Vitaly Kobyshysh were all interviewed by Bryant.

Michael Pressman *(special events producer):*

❝ In Moscow everything goes through the Soviet broadcasting. You have to get permission from them; everything had to be set up in advance and they would always send someone with you. In Moscow, if they say yes or no, they mean it. Once they say they will do something, they will bend over backward to do it—they make sure you have what you need. We were very understaffed in Moscow. We all pitched in and worked around the clock. ❞

Bryant in Moscow and Jane in New York were brilliant. Everyone on the *Today* team was ecstatic, and the *Today* audiences were impressed; the ratings showed it.

Larry Grossman:

❝ The Moscow trip was a tremendous success. It was a great gamble for the network, and I

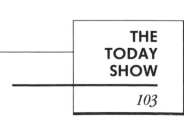

am proud they went along with it. We had not a single interview lined up when *Today* left for Moscow. There was a tremendous amount of money at stake. It was a real departure from anything *Today* had done before.
We got very lucky! **"**

GERRY DAVIS

TODAY TODAY

Critics were now rewording their critiques, and viewers were watching intently. Bryant was not the sharp, curt, brash, know-it-all, sarcastic, ridiculing, quick-to-put-you-down interviewer of earlier days. He was more receptive to others. His quickness and intelligence was not flaunted. He would let someone tell a story in his own way and his own words, even if it was not quite the way he would do it. He was beginning, as hard as it was, to *listen* to those who were not the superstars, whether it be in sports, politics, or life-styles. Bryant was mellowing well.

Gene Shalit, Jane Pauley, John Palmer, Bryant Gumbel, Willard Scott

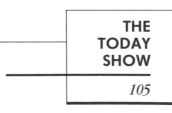

THE
TODAY
SHOW

105

Jane was more attractive than ever and had become a good interviewer. She could put people at ease. She herself was more at ease. She displayed a new self-assurance and confidence. She remained a very private person, but she had developed a relaxed and maternal demeanor. Guests felt at home with her. Her Indianian openness, wholesomeness, and naturalness now had a touch of big-city chic. It was appreciated.

CONTRIBUTORS

Contributors present more in-depth reports on various topics and have always been an important part of the *Today* show. Topics range from the serious to the frivolous. Over the years, there have been numerous contributors, some who have withstood the test of time and television, and others whose contributions have been short-lived.

Art Ulene began his television career with the *Today* show in 1976. He was the first doctor on national television, and it would be impossible to estimate how many viewer-patients he has helped over the years.

Art Ulene:

❛ Originally, I was the researcher behind medical subjects on the local L.A. station, KNBC. Within a short time, I was asked to do the medical reports on the air. I failed the studio test. The news director, Bob Eaton, who is now West Coast bureau director, said, "You'll be all right, after you relax." After a year on the local station, I received a call from *Today.* I had never heard of or seen the show. I was an active surgeon, also a teacher at U.C.L.A., and was out of the house by six A.M. I watched the show once, and thought it ❜ would be fun and agreed to do it.

Dr. Art Ulene's segments subsequently became one of the most popular features on *Today*. He chooses topics that affect a lot of people and tries to offer the viewer something they can do for themselves, such as breast self-examination, early checks of skin moles, or how to do the Heimlich maneuver. Within a few weeks of his first appearance, he received hundreds of letters. As he says, the thank you's he now receives daily in the mail are the ultimate reward.

Art Ulene:

❛ I offered a headache tip sheet. Within three days we received a hundred sixty thousand letters. It

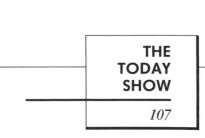

Dr. Art Ulene

was wild. The post office complained that they had not been warned—as if I had! They immediately gave me my own box and zip code. With the help of my family, friends, office staff, everyone, we answered all the letters. 🙂

Whatever your morning mood, when a Mike Leonard segment is completed you will probably be smiling. He roams the country "in search of what interests me." Leonard's segments reaffirm that you are normal and not alone with your quirky experiences, whether with vanishing socks or static cling. *Leave It to Beaver, My Three Sons,* and *Rocky and Bullwinkle* were his favorite TV shows; he hasn't watched much TV since.

Mike has happiness in his life, shares it, and practices what he preaches. "Make the most of every minute." Asked how he would like to be remembered, he says, "As a good daddy," but viewers will remember him as a reporter who may be referred to as "off beat" but who actually is very much "on beat" and in tempo.

Mike Leonard:

🙂 **I dropped my pants for Jane Pauley. It was shortly after having a shamrock tatooed on my butt—my father and three brothers were similarly branded, and I was eager to show it off. I told Jane that I had something to show her, and before she knew it I was unbuckling my pants. We were alone in a small office, and I could see that she was starting to get nervous—panic, actually. Great relief spread over her face when it was the shamrock that was unveiled and nothing else.**

Another wonderful moment came when Bryant announced the birth of our fourth child. I was visiting my wife in the hospital at the time, holding Brendan and watching the show. We'll show him the videotape when he's old enough to understand. It may sound corny, but there's a sense of family on *Today* and that moment just strengthened it for me.

Once I did a feature report on the presidential Christmas card and why I never received one. After all, seventy thousand were mailed out to dignitaries, statesmen, members of the press, and so on. After the story aired, Christmas cards jammed my mailbox from all over the country. The story was meant in fun, but the messages that I received were heartwarming and sympathetic. A typical one read, "We're not important people, nor do we live in a

fancy white house, but we do wish that you and your family have a nice Christmas." Cards arrived from people in all walks of life—convicts, children, grandmothers, families, other newspeople. I sent cards back to them, and now our family Christmas card list has been expanded to **9** include people we've never met.

When you ask someone for a job description and he says he is a correspondent covering science, technology, medicine, the sex life of alligators, and advances in particle physics, you might naturally wonder what he thinks about at a stoplight or in the shower. **Bob Bazell,** who has been science correspondent for *Today* since 1980, presents a segment that could fit any of these categories every Monday morning. You know he understands his subject because when his segment is over, you feel as if you understand it.

There is not another job he would want aside from the one he has, but he does wish it were not in the morning. But it's worth it to report live from the space shuttle launches (twenty-one in all), or from the vast expanses of White Sands, New Mexico, or from outside the operating room as Barney Clark gets the first artificial heart.

Bob Bazell:

❛ The best thing about *Today* is the mixture of people you meet because of it. It is wonderful to appear on the show between a movie star and some convicted criminal and to get **9** the chance to meet them both.

Owner of two Golden Retriever dogs, one cat, one rabbit, one horse, and one Reisse turtle (about the size of a medium grapefruit), David Horowitz would like to be president of the United States of America, but until that fantasy materializes, he loves every minute of his "hectic, high-energy job" as consumer commentator on *Today*. "A good day is any day you get up and go to work."

He has one gripe, however, about *Today,* and that's not having a set to work out of in Los Angeles that measures up to what he works out of in New York.

Horowitz has presented some extremely informative and original consumer reports on topics such as Samsonite luggage and which brand of spaghetti sauce really tastes homemade. He hopes he is thought of as someone who has made a contribution to public awareness. He has.

David Horowitz

Alberta Hunter and Gene Shalit

Betty Furness's career has spanned many facets of show business. After graduating from a prestigious college, she went on to be a model, then an actress in Hollywood, where she made over thirty-five movies. In New York, Betty became known to millions in the early years of television as the "Westinghouse Lady." Becoming involved in TV news, she covered the 1964 national conventions as a political reporter for CBS. By 1975, Betty Furness had joined NBC, where she became consumer affairs director of *NewsCenter 4*. Previous to that she had been chief consumer advocate for the president of the United States, the state of New York, and the city of New York.

By 1976, Betty frequently appeared on *Today* in a variety of spots, primarily consumer-oriented, ranging from a report on the inability of postal machines to check correct postage to a report on the problem of ill-fitting fitted sheets. With selections from her own wardrobe, she has shown how a beautiful dress she once wore in a movie or an Easter bonnet of the fifties exemplifies that "the more things change, the more they stay the same." Except, of course, in craftsmanship and price.

Movies, theater, and other aspects of entertainment are reviewed from **Gene Shalit**'s private turf, the Critic's Corner, the set of which resembles his real office. Shalit has been described as "that man in the morning with a head of hair like an untended vineyard and a mustache bigger than a hedgerow."

Since 1973, Gene's barbed remarks and wisecracks—not prone to kitchen hobbies, he once said in an interview with Paul Newman, "I don't cook. I thaw and I eat out"—have given way to more tolerance and sincerity. A baseball enthusiast and a man whose large vocabulary runs from the printable to the unprintable, Gene Shalit is the *Today* show's favorite eccentric.

Michael Jensen has been reporting on business and economics for NBC since 1978. His weekly feature on *Today*, originally called *Staying Afloat*, later *The Jen$en Report*, focuses on the complicated world of finance and takes complex issues and presents them in an understandable yet in-depth manner.

Bob Jamieson became an NBC News correspondent in 1971. From presidential candidates to civil violence in Northern Ireland to the conflict in the Falklands to substituting on *Today* for John Palmer, Bob has reported on a wide spectrum of topics and places.

Eight years ago, as a news rookie, **Ken Bode** was told by Tom Brokaw, "Work for *Today*. They have a political audience, and you can present the news as you see it." Four years ago, Ken presented the idea of *Bode's Journal* to Steve Friedman. Steve said that they would try it for a month. It worked.

Bode's Journal presents the hard facts along with the amusing or ironic aspects of the story. However, regardless of the slant, Ken is quick to point out, the television picture is what really tells the story.

Along with Ken Bode, political analysts **David Broder** and **Jack Germond** are also frequent contributors to *Today,* providing insightful comments on the domestic and international political climates. Combined with veteran political advisors **John Sears** and **Bob Squire,** the impressive savvy of this group gives the *Today* viewer a leading edge into the world and local political scene.

Jon Alpert is a reporter *extraordinaire.* Regularly seen on *Today,* his segments are informative, revealing and, at times, close to unbelievable. Whether reporting from Vietnam, New York's Bowery, South America, or Harlem, the viewer watches in amazement and wonders, "How does he get such incredible footage?"

Jon won an Emmy for his investigative reporting on hard metals disease, another one for his coverage from Nicaragua. His report about a woman squatter in Philadelphia who had done a wonderful job of fixing up an abandoned building aired the day before it was to be auctioned off. Due to the report, the building was saved, and a new housing policy was instituted in Philadelphia.

Jon Alpert:

❧ If Steve had not been executive producer, I would probably have been thrown overboard a long, long time ago. Initially, due to Tom Brokaw, I was first on NBC and then, due to Steve, I went on *Today.* For all the people who like our reports, there are many who see them differently, ❜ but the mail does run ten to one in favor.

Pat Mitchell is a contributor twice each month with "Woman to Woman on *Today.*" Her pieces usually include four or five guests whom she guides through intimate conversations on topics such as date rape, single fathers, or women who made conscience choices to become and remain single mothers.

Roaming the country to glean material for his "Cross Country" segments, **Boyd Matson** finds and presents not only human-interest stories but also the bizarre, such as the Da Free John

Jim Brown with Orson Welles and Barbara Leaming

Joe Witte

religious cult. He began his career as a disk jockey while still in college in Oklahoma, but then went on to Texas and Los Angeles where he was reporter/cameraman, weekend co-anchor, daily sportscaster, sports director, and writer, producer, and host of sports specials. His easy-going manner contributes to making "Cross Country" a popular *Today* segment.

Jim Brown, *Today*'s "man in Hollywood" has been with the show since 1979. He covers the Hollywood personalities—the box-office stars, past and present, the character actors who flourished in the 1930s and 1940s, the producers and directors, the stuntmen and women . . . and practically every possible (and presentable!) aspect of the Hollywood scene.

Joe Witte, meteorologist and substitute for Willard Scott, has been with *Today* for over three years. His daily assignment is weatherman on NBC's *News at Sunrise,* but he averages close to fifty days a year on *Today* filling in for Willard. Mr. Witte is definitely an erudite meteorologist who will tell you exactly why the sky is blue.

Nancy Foreman: blond, petite, wife, mother, jogger, skiier, and for some six years one of the life-style correspondent and commercial spokeswoman on *Today.* She is also the author of *Bound for Success,* a book of advice on getting the most out of oneself, one's career, and one's relationships.

Nancy produces and presents segments covering a variety of topics, such as what's new in the furniture world, that often take her out of the studio and on location across America. As commercial spokeswoman, she frequently has had to deal with props and animals, as in Alpo commercials, which she accomplishes with a bright smile.

In November 1984, Linda Ellerbee became a regular weekly contributor to *Today.* Linda had covered the House of Representatives for NBC; had co-anchored *Weekend,* the news magazine, with Lloyd Dobbins; had been co-anchor and editor of NBC's *Overnight*; had co-anchored *Summer Sunday, USA*; had produced special projects for *Nightly News,* and now, for *Today,* had created *T.G.I.F.* As of this writing, Linda Ellerbee is considering other avenues for her career.

Linda Ellerbee:

❝ I invented *T.G.I.F.* but when asked to describe it, I said, "I don't know *what* it is, but I know *when* it is." ❞

Linda admits she works best when trying new things and "pushing the edges." Because of advances with satellite technology, the feeds of every kind of material that never before was available now makes a segment like *T.G.I.F.* possible. It contains a little bit about a lot of things that cause viewers to ponder, then smile.

Linda Ellerbee:

❝ T.G.I.F. just comes out of the sky. The video editor and I are video doctors. We take the stuff, put it together, and make it better—and so it goes. ❞

EXPOSURE

On that first *Today* Monday in 1952 in the RCA Exhibition Hall, author Fleur Cowles was interviewed about her new book, *Bloody Precedent.* In the brief four minutes she was on the air, Cowles was so effective in plugging her book that it became a goal for others in the publishing world to appear on the *Today* show.

Considering the number of viewers an author can reach in a few minutes, heated competition to get on the air is understandable. Figure in that if a publisher were to purchase those minutes, it would cost in the neighborhood of $100,000.

Emily Boxer is the current book editor of *Today* and has been with the show seven years. She works closely with the publishers. With over three thousand books published each month, only a lucky three hundred a year are chosen.

Dave Garroway with Alben Barkley

Emily Boxer:

❻ **Often the author who is chatty and outgoing and interesting on the phone chokes on camera.** ❾

In January 1985, *Today* celebrated its thirty-third anniversary. During the anniversary show, this trivia quiz was given (answers follow):

1. What event caused the first overnight program change on *Today* three weeks after its premiere?
2. During the days when *Today* had windows on Forty-ninth Street, a man dressed as a gorilla held up a sign that read I'M J. FRED MUGGS'S LONG LOST BROTHER. What did the sign's flip side read?
3. What was the site of *Today*'s first week-long trip abroad?
4. What overseer of Massachusetts General Hospital appeared on *Today* to commemorate the hospital's 150th anniversary?
5. NBC News correspondent John Chancellor replaced host Dave Garroway in July 1961. Prior to joining *Today*, where was Chancellor based?
6. What was Barbara Walters's first major on-air assignment for *Today*?
7. In 1965, *Today* became the first regularly scheduled program

ever transmitted by space satellite. What was the satellite's name?

8. What was the first full year *Today* was telecast in color?
9. What was the name of the sister of J. Fred Muggs?
10. Which star of the blockbuster movie *Ghostbusters* is the offspring of the founder of *Today*?
11. What well-known actress was *Today*'s first "gal Friday"?

Answers

1. The death of England's King George VI
2. TONIGHT WATCH *King Kong* ON CHANNEL 9.
3. Paris
4. President John F. Kennedy
5. Moscow
6. Jacqueline Kennedy's goodwill tour of India
7. The early-bird satellite
8. 1966
9. Phoebe B. Beebe
10. Sigourney Weaver, daughter of Sylvester "Pat" Weaver
11. Estelle Parsons

For the scoring, give yourself five points for each correct answer, but take away three for each wrong one.

50–55 POINTS	A mind like a steel trap
40–49 POINTS	You either worked for *Today* or you wish you did
20–39 POINTS	Not bad, just a little rusty
0–19 POINTS	You either worked nights or couldn't wake up
−33– 0 POINTS	Either senility or youth is your undoing

There was nothing trivial about the *Today* shows in 1985. Viewers, critics, and networks were now taking new notice. The ingredients were there, and they were finally working not individually but as a team. The soufflé was about to rise. Steve Friedman had been right and had done it!

ON THE ROAD

In 1985, a travel marathon began for *Today* . . . first stop, Italy. It was not the first time *Today* had been to Rome, but now the show could be broadcast live. It was Easter week and on March 27, 1985, during Wednesday's regularly scheduled public audience at the Vatican, Pope John Paul II welcomed NBC's *Today.*

Pope John Paul II:

❝ I am particularly pleased to welcome the group from the American television network NBC, which will be broadcasting directly to the United States from the Vatican during Holy Week. It is my hope that your work will bear much spiritual fruit during this holy season when Christians all over the world celebrate the death and resurrection of Jesus Christ. Through you I send warm and cordial greetings to all the people of America. ❞

Few events have meant more to *Today* staffers than what they experienced and shared with viewers on Monday, April 1, 1985, from Rome.

Tim Russert (vice-president and assistant to the president of NBC News):

❝ We went to the Vatican and into the Pauline Chapel, the Pope's private chapel. Suddenly, he walked in. It was a bonding of Christians and Jews and blacks and whites. It was the *Today* show at its finest. ❞

In a network television first, His Holiness Pope John Paul II celebrated a special televised mass for the staff of NBC's *Today.* It was the first time the Pauline Chapel had been opened to television cameras. The mass was partially broadcast, live, during the first hour of *Today.* Coverage from Rome included topics such as terrorism and politics.

Pope John Paul II

Tim Russert:

❦ It was on the Rome program that President Bertinni announced he wasn't running for re-election. We began to sense that the *Today* show was not only an American institution but ❞ was developing an international reputation.

Also covered were Americans playing football and basketball in Italy, and fashion.

On April 1, the curator of the Colosseum arrived there to view wood mannequins in evening gowns scheduled to be used later that day in an interview with fashion designer Valentino. The curator refused to let them remain, yelling in Italian, "There will be no dummies in my Colosseum!" Four hours later, after arguing and cajoling he still would not let the "dummies" remain. It was

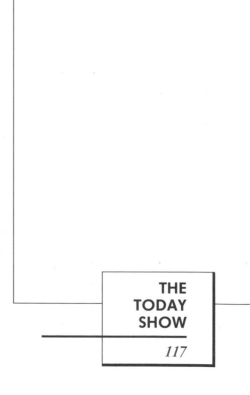

one in the afternoon, an hour before air time, and he went off for his three-hour lunch break [7 to 9 A.M. New York time is 2 to 4 P.M. Rome time]. While he was gone, the mannequins were re-dressed, used, and removed. When the curator returned, there were indeed no dummies in the Colosseum. So much for April Fool's Day in Rome.

Other topics discussed on the air were Italy's underground economy and the relationship between church and state.

Cheryl Wells:

❦ Michelle Berg and I were to escort the guests onto the stage at the Colosseum on cue from the stage manager, Jim Straka. We each had three guests. We're talking about important guests, like cardinals and the religious people whose hands everyone was kissing. Michelle had the first guest and escorted him out. Then it was my turn. We got the cue from Straka and walked out from under the column, and the famous pigeons of Rome scored a direct hit on this poor man's head. He just stood there in shock. We ran and got towels, but it was still all over him and he went on live television with bird——— all over him. Then it was Michelle's turn. Nothing happened. Now it was my turn, and Straka gave us the cue. Out we went, and again the pigeons found the guest! Michelle went with her third guest and nothing happened. It was my turn again, and Jeff Hark, the unit manager, got me an umbrella. I was standing there with this umbrella over the guest. I don't think anything happened the third time, but it was the most hysterical thing because you couldn't do anything about it. ❧
You had to go on air right then!

Peter Ustinov, the actor, was seen dressed as Emperor Nero; Joseph LaPalomba, Susanna Agnelli, Gore Vidal, Millicent Fenwick, and Claudia Cardinale were among the featured guests.

Today's Rome trip was a huge success. Critics and viewers praised what they saw. Wonderful Willard Scott got right to the point when he said from the Colosseum, "Friends, Romans, countrymen! I come to bury David Hartman, not to praise him."

Tim Russert:

❦ There were many special unscripted moments. At one point, the Pope asked Willard if he was

from Philadelphia, and Willard said, "No, I'm a Baptist." The Pope roared with laughter, truly enjoying it. Willard said later, "That Pope, he's my kind of guy."

The *Today* show reaffirmed itself as "the best of the morning shows and a great American institution." We came home knowing we had done something special. 〝

YEAR OF THE COMEBACK FOR NBC NEWS
—*Broadcasting* magazine

In traveling to Rome and in landing perhaps the world's most coveted guest, the *Today* show reaffirmed itself as the best of the morning shows and a great American institution.
—*The Washington Post*

When *Today* finished its five days of broadcasting from Rome, it had managed to gain unusual access to an institution historically wary of news and television organizations.
—*The New York Times*

From Rome, *Today* went to Ho Chi Minh City, where Bryant anchored *Today* live on the tenth anniversary of the American withdrawal from Vietnam.

For most viewers, Ho Chi Minh City was a name that evoked thoughts of war and a time in America's history that was anything but memorable. It was also a place that would rarely be on one's holiday travel itinerary. Bryant's excellent reporting only served to underscore what Steve Friedman had believed about Bryant. *Today*'s coverage was without flaws, but it had flies. It was nighttime in Ho Chi Minh City when *Today* aired in New York, and lights were needed on Bryant's set. The lights attracted flies by the swarms, making it most unpleasant for Bryant, as well as the crew. In spite of the annoyances, *Today* once again brought to its viewers a part of the world few will ever see firsthand.

Highlights of *Today*'s historic week in Vietnam included a lengthy interview by Bryant with Le Duc Tho, who discussed the reestablishment of relations with the United States. "We pose no preconditions for normalization," Tho said, "and we believe the United States should not either."

Jane Pauley's broadcast on April 29 from the Vietnam Memorial in Washington, D.C., was designed to coordinate with Bryant's in

Ho Chi Minh City and to measure the impact of "America's Longest War" on the United States. Back in the studio, her interviews included discussions with senators who were Vietnam veterans; Graham Martin, the last U.S. ambassador to Vietnam; three women who served in Vietnam; and Jan Scruggs and Robert Muller, who were responsible for the erection of the Vietnam Memorial.

Today from Vietnam was transmitted via satellite to the United States by use of an exclusive NBC ground station installed in Ho Chi Minh City.

"All Aboard," and that is just what *Today* did, taking a specially equipped Amtrak train from Houston to New Orleans, Memphis, Indianapolis, and Cincinnati. From May 20 to May 24, 1985, the *Today* Express took its viewers through the heartlands of America, beginning in Houston, Texas.

Preparing the Amtrak train for the *Today* Express caravan was not an overnight accomplishment. Aside from all the usual needs, this time *Today* was going to be riding the rails, and the staff had to learn all about trains and train travel and arrange the facilities not only on board, but also at the various stops along the way.

*Peter Ustinov and Bryant Gumbel
in Rome*

Jeff Hark:

❛ Where were we going to get the power from to transmit on a train? You have to duplicate almost to the Nth degree everything that exists within our controlled environ- ❜ ment in the New York studio.

Michael Pressman:

❛ We have a travel pack, which in essence is a portable control room. We can put it in a truck, in a hotel—this time ❜ we put it on a train.

Jeff Hark:

❛ When we took the train trip, Amtrak insisted that we carry an enormous amount of insurance coverage. "Supposing the train hits a tractor-trailer, or a school bus, God forbid, at a crossing gate?" Amtrak said. "We're not in charge. It is your train, you rented it, and we're going at your direction. If we hit a school bus stalled in front of a car,

**that's your insurance problem, fella, not Amtrak's."
So we had to work out incredible
insurance contracts for that trip.**

By the time the Amtrak-*Today* Express pulled into New Orleans, the staff knew more about trains than they ever thought possible.

In Houston, Mayor Kathy Whitmire talked about the city's economic recovery. Phylicia Ayers-Allen (now Phylicia Ashad), co-star of *The Cosby Show* and a Houston native, shared some of her childhood memories with Jane and Bryant. Boxcar Willie, the singer and composer; Alan Bean, former astronaut turned artist; Maxine Messinger, society columnist; and twelve-year-old Brian Zimmerman, mayor of Crabb, Texas, also appeared. The value and future of America's rail system was debated by Graham Claytor, president of Amtrak, and Fred Smith, transportation expert and critic. As the train prepared to depart for its next stop, New Orleans, the Houston Rhythm Cloggers performed.

On Tuesday, the *Today* Express pulled into New Orleans, Bryant's birthplace. New Orleans' mayor, Ernest "Dutch" Morial, presented Jane and Bryant with keys to the city and declared May 21 "Bryant Gumbel Day," a day on which Bryant could do anything but "violate the law." This was followed by a tour of New Orleans, a peek at some baby photos of Bryant and an introduction to two of his aunts, a chat with chef Paul Prudhomme, and Bryant's demonstration of how to eat crawfish. Mike Leonard presented the first edition of his "Train Diary," about overnighting on a moving train.

It was stormy as the *Today* Express pulled into Memphis on Wednesday. Only briefly did the rains stop—just long enough for Jerry Lee Lewis to present a mini-concert. Due to the rain, viewers were allowed an unscheduled look inside the train, where Jane and Bryant did most of the interviews. The Memphis show included an interview with senators Albert Gore, Sr., and Jr., and a discussion of Memphis's biggest attraction, Elvis Presley, and an interview with romance novelist Virginia Brown. Finally, there was a discussion of the resurgence of steam engines, with two railroad employees, J. W. Vinson, conductor, and Charles Carruthers, engineer, looking back at the changes in train travel and recalling the allure and mystery of train life.

From Memphis they continued on to Indianapolis, where Mayor William Hudnut proclaimed "Jane Pauley Day" and made Bryant an honorary citizen. Willard was presented with a loaf of bread in the shape of an Indy 500 race car. Jane had a surprise visit from some of her childhood friends and her high school speech teacher, and viewers saw tapes of Jane's home and school and a picture from her high school yearbook. Dr. June Reinisch, director of the Kinsey Institute; Indiana's Lieutenant Governor John Mutz; and Peter Sterling, director of the Indianapolis Children's Museum; were among the guests.

On Friday, the *Today* Express stopped at Yeatman's Cove in Cincinnati. Featured were the Ohio Savings and Loan situation, Ohio tourism, Bill Yunker, who runs a non-profit children's television network, Cincinnati's fight to keep out the porn industry, and guests Pete Rose and Johnny Bench.

Michael Pressman:

❝ The train trip was very enjoyable. Technical problems aside, everyone was very cooperative. People met us at each stop. There was a real feeling of intimacy. It was exciting—it worked. We should do more of these shows. ❞

As *Today* traveled, *Today* attracted the viewers. *Today* was looking good in the ratings race.

What Steve Friedman had set out to do, what the NBC executives had wanted, was happening. The pace of the show had quickened, the interviews and segments had been lengthened, everyone was listening, and the players were working as a team.

Jane Pauley *(NBC news release):*

❝ The atmosphere around here ❞ is restrained euphoria.

Many people had commented that "something changed" when *Today* moved from the showcase to an inside studio at NBC. It was an understandable move, but it was too bad it had to be done. But for one night on August 19, 1985, *Today* went back "on the street." Jane, Bryant, and Willard, along with Gene Shalit and John Palmer, were in the Channel Gardens at Rockefeller Center along with an assembled crowd to present *Today at Night.*

Guests included Speaker of the House Tip O'Neill, Don Johnson and Philip Michael Thomas of *Miami Vice,* and three-year-old Trina Engerbretsen and her mother, Mary Ann. Trina and her mother had appeared on *Today* in January 1984 in a successful plea for a liver donor for Trina. The Goodyear blimp *America* provided views of the Manhattan skyline. Willard Scott's stops across the country as the program's "Goodwill Ambassador" were spotlighted, and John Palmer took a look at major news events of the past year.

The Today *train*

Today at Night: *Jane Pauley, Bryant Gumbel, Willard Scott, and John Palmer in the Channel Gardens*

Barbara Walters:

❝ *Today at Night* was not a first. I remember we did a program at night and the reason I remember it so well was that I had just had a miscarriage. I got home from the hospital that day and did the show that night—like a damn fool. It was so important to me to be on at night. I didn't have a car and I remember standing on the corner trying to get a cab. I couldn't run. I remember thinking, "I am out of my mind." The show went ❞ on at seven and I had to be there at five.

Changes had occurred in virtually every aspect of *Today,* including the offices. And now, yet another change, a new musical theme by award-winning composer and Boston Pops conductor John Williams.

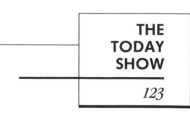

THE
TODAY
SHOW

Tom Wolzien *(vice-president, editorial and productions services):*

❝ **No news organization has commissioned a serious piece of music like this from a composer of the caliber of John Williams. We are happy to replace the synthesizer "news noise" with the world-class composition John has written for us.** ❞

On Friday, September 13, 1985, John Williams introduced the new theme on *Today*. Musically, the theme was powerful and certainly more contemporary than its predecessor. There were, though, a few complaints. It was not really a humming tune, for example. Upon hearing it you expected to see something awesome occur, a possible parting of the sea or golden lights in the sky. One viewer pleaded, "Please bring back the *bing bong bing!*"

Considering what was going on at *Today*, perhaps the new theme was perfectly suited, it just took a little bit of getting used to.

Steve Friedman:

❝ **We've caught up to them now and we intend to win.** ❞

The *Today* show had listened, asked, looked, learned, and tried, and now it was ready to be the best—again. *Today* was celebrating its thirty-fourth anniversary in January 1986, and because it had recently topped *GMA* in the ratings five times, there was good reason to celebrate.

But the critics were at it again, particularly at the offices of the competition. They were quick to point out that tremendous amounts of money had been spent on travel and promotions by NBC.

Steve Friedman:

❝ **All the promotion in the world doesn't do any good if you don't back it up with good programming. You can't buy an audience.** ❞

Today was giving a tremendous amount of enjoyment to its viewers. For the anniversary show, there was a colorful retrospective of highlights of past shows.

Steve Friedman:

❝ We're caretakers of American broadcasting history. It has to be as great for the next thirty-four years as it has been for the last thirty-four. ❞

On January 20, 1986, *Today* celebrated the first national Martin Luther King, Jr., holiday and featured an exclusive interview with Coretta Scott King. Also on the show were rock star Stevie Wonder, who had been a major lobbyist for the establishment of the national holiday; Mayor Andrew Young of Atlanta; and *Today* correspondent Richard Valeriani, who presented a look at some of the people who surrounded Dr. King in the sixties.

Mrs. Coretta Scott King and Dr. Martin Luther King, Sr.

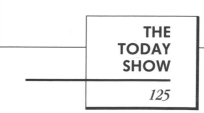

TOUCHDOWN

Travel was again on the agenda of *Today* in 1986 with its kickoff to New Orleans for Super Bowl XX. A trip to New Orleans, the city of superb foods, dining, jazz music—that's work? The work was to get the remote on the air in spite of the fabulous distractions!

On the Thursday before the game, Bryant reported from the Superdome where he interviewed NFL commissioner Pete Rozelle and Super Bowl quarterbacks Jim McMahon of the Chicago Bears and Tony Eason of the New England Patriots. Also in New Orleans was correspondent Ken Bode, who explained the history and origins of Louisiana's Cajuns.

Friday's show was full of excited anticipation. Jane and Willard had joined Bryant in New Orleans and the program was broadcast from the fifty-yard line of the Superdome. Varying aspects of football were the topics. They included Mike Jensen's look at the eco-

Jane Pauley, Bryant Gumbel, and Willard Scott at the Super Bowl

nomics of the Super Bowl and Mike Leonard's witty perspective of how the Super Bowl would be telecast.

Of course, there were predictions of who would win the game. For the Bears, Chicago native Bryant: "The Patriots have peaked." Chicago's Steve Friedman: "Bears, twenty-seven to four-teen." George Paul, director, also from Chicago: "Bears, one hundred to zero." Senior producer, Marty Ryan, born and raised in Chicago: "Bears twenty-four, Patriots seven."

For the Patriots, Jane and John and Gene.

Final score, Bears 46, Patriots 10.

On Monday *Today* wrapped up Super Bowl XX from inside the Superdome. Featured were players from the winning Chicago Bears, a personal view by New Orleans native John Larroquette, a Mike Leonard piece, and jazz greats Al Hirt and Pete Fountain.

Slightly overfed, over-jazzed, and overtired, *Today* headed back to New York.

The *Today* staff had hardly lost the roar in their ears of the crowd at the Super Bowl, when on Tuesday, January 28, 1986, the space shuttle *Challenger* exploded!

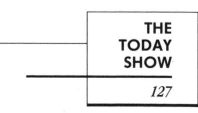

CRISES

When major news events like this occur, the *Today* plan for the next day is canceled and a completely new show is prepared. It is a massive job for the entire staff. New scripts must be written, tapes edited, and live interviews planned.

In this case the guests included: Christa McAuliffe's pastor, Reverend Chester Mrowka; two of McAuliffe's neighbors; former astronauts Alan Bean and David Scott; senators Jake Garn and Peter Domenici; a spokesperson for NASA's Young Astronauts Program who had been at the launch site; former director of the Johnson Space Center Gerald Griffin; Duke University Professor of Technology Alex Roland; and child psychologist Dr. Donna Gaffney, who discussed helping children cope with the tragedy. It is at a time like this that teamwork is put into overdrive. All types of arrangements must be made immediately. Often, it can result in hours of extended broadcasting and endurance tests for the entire staff.

Steve Friedman:

❝ **The American appetite for news has increased dramatically. On *Today* our philosophy is to cover big news live and to stay with it until it's resolved.** ❞

Eight and a half hours of expanded coverage—a record—occurred when Egyptian President Anwar Sadat was assassinated.

Max Schindler (Washington News Bureau):

❝ **It was very impressive—we stayed on the air until three P.M. keeping up with the events of Anwar Sadat's assassination.** ❞

Barbara Lyons (researcher):

❝ **The morning Sadat was killed we stayed on the air till the afternoon, and I was in the green room. We were running to the elevators to meet**

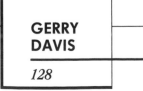

political and Mideast V.I.P.s, rushing them to makeup, and putting them into a chair on the set so Tom Brokaw could have someone to talk to while the situation got worse and worse. **"**

Unexpected events of great news magnitude are really never planned, so *Today* is always on call, much like a doctor in the emergency room, to cover the news as it happens on their shift. Over the years the *Today* staff, when learning of a major story, automatically heads for the office to be on hand and help get the news on the air.

Susan Butler Miles:

" You get so involved with the show that the news element almost takes precedence over anything else. The evening that Martin Luther King was assassinated, I was on my way home and, hearing the news, I just turned around and went back to the office. Personal grief is **"** put aside for the show.

Another example of instant change and additions to a planned show occurred when President Leonid Brezhnev died.

Marty Ryan (senior producer):

" We were planning a long show for Thursday, November 11, 1982, because of a space shuttle launch. When the death of Soviet President Leonid Brezhnev was announced the same day, we covered both stories and **"** were on the air until noon.

Throughout a crisis, NBC News keeps a phone line or lines open continuously. For the coverage of TWA flight 847's hijacking, lines were open from Beirut to the NBC London Bureau, and updates were aired every half hour along with hotline reports when the situation warranted. *Today* aired a special edition on Monday, devoting most of the program to the plight of the passengers and crew. All weekend staff was on hand obtaining information and tapes, writing, editing, and booking pertinent guests. With the total change of the Monday show, all the scheduled segments and planned reports for the following days were affected.

Marty Ryan:

❝ *Today's* hallmark has been its ability to revise an entire program around late-breaking news events. This is what we live for. When a big story is happening, like the *Challenger* explosion, you feel the energy level in the control room rise. Everyone makes the extra effort to be on top of the day's event. ❞

Tom Brokaw:

❝ There was always such a festive air at launch time. Quite honestly, I had been concerned that the shuttle would blow up on us. I didn't know the O-ring problem, or anything like that, but I knew the danger was there. I would talk with the astronauts that we were working with and say, "Now if something goes wrong, I am counting on you to talk about it in scientific terms, not get emotional." It used to worry me. You know when that thing takes off it is so emotional, so exhilarating—I always thought that we could never adequately convey to the television audience what it was like to be there. ❞

Bryant Gumbel was on vacation when the tragedy occurred. He called Steve Friedman to find out if he wanted him to return for the special edition of the show. The answer was no. Bryant deserved a vacation, and the staff could handle the show.

This episode illustrates several qualities of *Today* professionals: Bryant's concern for the show, Steve's acknowledgment that Bryant was human and couldn't be on the show every day, and that the entire staff is always "on call" and gets the job done.

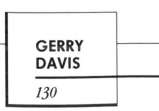

GERRY DAVIS

130

SOUTH AMERICA

Surveys, research, and remote planning surveys had all taken place, and as February 1986 started, the New York *Today* offices were virtually empty. Practically everyone was in South America for a week of broadcasting from Rio de Janeiro, Brazil, and Buenos Aires, Argentina.

Jeff Hark:

 **The South America trip was almost double the cost of the Rome trip. It cost a lot more to get there and more to ship the equipment. In Brazil you couldn't just go into the country and do work. We had to pay to get visas, money that was supposedly passed on to the trade unions in Brazil. They asked for ten percent of my salary for every day I worked in Brazil. So every NBC person who went down there paid ten percent of base salary up front to the Brazilian government for every day he or she worked.**

The cost of shipping the equipment was astronomical. In both Brazil and Argentina it was confiscated as it landed. After you pay the brokers to make sure that doesn't happen, it happens anyway. Then it takes a week or two to get it out of customs!

Michael Pressman:

 **It was the very hardest remote. No one knew the *Today* show. Although the people were very nice, they were skeptical about us, and there were subtle hostilities. There is a wealth of wonderful things in Brazil. There was no problem coming up with ideas, but the execution was very hard.**

On Friday, February 7, 1986, the first day of the city's Carnival celebrations, Bryant broadcasted live from Rio de Janeiro. Segments included an interview with the U.S. ambassador to Brazil,

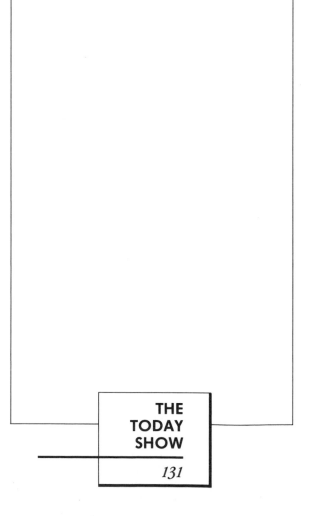

Diego Cortes Asencio, and a talk with famed plastic surgeon Dr. Ivo Pitanguy. Boyd Matson presented a report on the ecology of the Amazon region, and Bob Jamieson gave a preview of his report from Antarctica.

Michael Pressman:

Finding guests who were willing to come in during Carnival was hard. A typical *Today* show guest who lived in Rio was going to try to get as far away as possible during Carnival. We had to really convince people to stay. It was a miracle, every guest we wanted on the show showed up. It was also a miracle we got the show on the air.

Today in South America got off to an excellent start. Viewers could tell that extensive preparations had been made. The week was sure to be one of the most interesting *Today* trips.

On Monday, February 10, Jane and Willard joined Bryant. Throughout the week telecasts were done from various locations around Rio. On Monday, the program originated from the Sambodromo. Among the many interviewed that day were soccer legend Pelé; popular singer Antonio Carlos Jobim, famed for his composition "The Girl from Ipanema"; and sportswriter Joao Saldanha.

On Tuesday, the Copacabana Beach was the *Today* set. Segments included looks at the Amazon River; Villa Americana, a Brazilian town settled by Americans just after the Civil War; and Rio's wild nightlife. *Today* viewers were taken on a visual tour of São Paulo and Brasilia. Other topics covered were the role of women in Brazil's macho society; Brazilian soap operas, which are viewed by 96 percent of the population; and Brazil's role as fifth-largest seller of arms in the world.

Reminiscent of the days in the RCA Exhibition Hall, when people would display signs with messages outside the window, six American teachers from the Chapel American School in São Paulo drove one hundred miles and waited for several hours on the beach before the *Today* telecast. They wanted to see the show, meet Willard, and hold up their sign for all their American friends and families to see: HI, MOM. SEND M&MS. They said life in Brazil was wonderful, but, "We have been dying for M&Ms and a good tortilla."

Today's final Brazilian telecast on Wednesday was from the Yacht Club of Rio de Janeiro with topics that included trade pro-

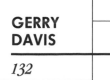

GERRY DAVIS

tectionism, the gem industry, and the encroachment of civilization on the Amazon Indians.

One of the special insights into South America was a segment produced by Lisa Freed who, with a two-man camera crew, went to the Amazon to live with the Kayapo Indians for five days. The Kayapos are primitive, but they are also the owners of a generator used to power the video equipment. Initially the Kayapo chief was unwilling to let the crew on the Kayapo reservation, but when Lisa Freed promised to give the tribe a copy of "their segment as aired on the *Today* show with introduction by Bryant Gumbel," the reservation was opened. At the suggestion of anthropologist Darrell Posey, who has studied the Kayapo tribe, Lisa Freed brought not only food supplies, videotapes, cameras, and battery packs, but also twelve kilos of glass beads, or *micanga,* imported from Czechoslovakia, which the Kayapos valued and wore proudly.

From Brazil *Today* traveled to Buenos Aires, where the Plaza de Mayo became the set for *Today.* One could not help but see and learn the differences between Brazil and Argentina. Tennis champion Guillermo Vilas took the viewers on a tour of Buenos Aires; there was a trip to Mount Fitzroy, the tallest peak in South America; and a Bob Jamieson report offered a surprising look at the advent of tourism in Antarctica (on tape, not quite yet a *Today* remote). Politics, sports, life among the gauchos, flirting Latin style, and pop-rock music were also presented.

The final *Today* in South America came from the Plaza San Martín in Buenos Aires. A fashion show featuring popular leather designs; the inhabitants of the city's nightclubs; a live performance by famed tango musician and composer Astor Piazzola; a visit with actress Julie Christie and co-star Nacha Guevara on the set of their movie, *Miss Maggie*; an in-depth look at the effect of the Falklands war on Argentinian youth, and more, were shared by *Today* and its audience.

On location in South America

Jeff Hark:

🌑 It is wonderful to be able to do the program in a country where they speak English. Their mindsets are similar to ours. In Brazil, they are definitely not. They have a different way of doing business, a different time clock. Doing it immediately could mean in the next hour, in the next day, or the next week. You say to the caterer in the hotel, "May I please have coffee for ten people on this table tomorrow morning at seven o'clock?" "No problem," he says. Now what does "no problem" mean? It means it'll be there, right? From our experience it means no

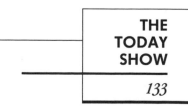

problem, I'll have it there tomorrow, maybe the day after, maybe next week or, no problem, my mother is fine. There is no correlation between what you ask for and what they said and whether what you asked for is what the execution will be. It was very difficult in Brazil. In Argentina it was just the opposite. You say you want X and you get X. **9**

THE PRODUCERS

Since *Today*'s first producers, Richard Pinkham and Mort Werner, there have been many who have filled that role. Steve Friedman has been executive producer of *Today* since May 1980.

According to *The New York Times Encyclopedia of Television*, a producer is a person in charge of a TV production who establishes the working spirit and dictates the standards to be met. Ideally, as head of the creative team, the producer is both businessman and artist, caring about the administration and budgetary details while nurturing the talent and providing the vision for the project.

Steve Friedman holds many awards—five Emmys between 1975 and 1977—but none resulted from anything more challenging than position as ninth executive producer of *Today*. Anyone can take over a show when it is on top, that's easy. But when he took over, ratings were precarious and the competition was stiff.

A native of Chicago, and an avid Chicago Cubs fan, Steve Friedman joined NBC in 1969 as a news writer for KNBC Los Angeles. In 1977, he was made associate producer of *Today* in Los Angeles.

Steve personifies the definition of producer. He also has the ability to see the center of an issue as well as its possible outer scopes. He listens. He makes decisions quickly. He has a way with words. He can be abrupt and brash at times, but he has a heart and a sense of humor.

Steve Friedman, executive producer

Tom Brokaw:

❝ Steve is the quintessential *Today* show executive producer. His range of interest is very wide, his energy is legendary, and his commitment is total. He's a little crazy, which also helps. ❞

In 1982, Marty Ryan became senior producer of *Today*. Associated with the show since 1977, he had been Midwest producer, based in his hometown of Chicago. His smile makes you wonder, but one thing is certain, he, too, is a Cubs fan!

Steve Friedman:

❝ Marty is a guy who is so demanding of himself that he does the job no matter how many hours it takes or how many days a week. He is always there, always answers the bell. ❞

Los Angeles-based associate producer for *Today* since 1980, Scott Goldstein came to New York and became a *Today* producer in 1982, and, in 1985, a supervising producer, responsible for "After 8" segments.

Steve Friedman:

❝ Scott's job is to come up with ideas that are not obvious. He is the guy who hopefully will get things on the show before they're in *Newsweek* and *Time*. He is a very innovative and creative guy. ❞

Cliff Kappler has been with NBC News since 1967. From 1976 to 1979, he was manager of Europe NBC News, based in London. In 1980, he joined *Today* as producer.

Cliff Kappler, producer, talking with Jane Pauley and Bryant Gumbel

Steve Friedman:

❝ Cliff is an interesting guy because he grew up through NBC. While Marty grew up in Chicago and in L.A. Cliff is New York born and bred. He knows a lot about the business here. He knows a lot about the organization, he knows where the bodies are buried. Cliff is a valuable guy. He knows about overseas; we are domestic types. He provides a very good balance. He is very much like Marty. That is why we call them Spinner and Marty; they got the nickname from *The Mickey Mouse Club.* ❞

Being the producer of the *Today* show is an unforgettable experience. To Al Morgan the *Today* years were marvelous years.

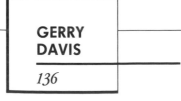

GERRY
DAVIS

136

Al Morgan:

❝ I have a plastic paperweight of horse manure, a major tourist item from Mackinac Island. I've slept on brocade couches in palaces, met killer whales, lost a fighting bull in the hills of Portugal, and spent a night with a bottle of wine and a loaf of bread on the Acropolis. I've walked the beaches of Puerto Rico with Pablo Casals and sat in his living room and listened to him practice. I have stood in the awesome silence of Anne Frank's bedroom.

There comes a time when you should leave, when you find yourself saying, "Oh damn, another opening, oh damn, another book." ❞

Joe Garagiola:

❝ Today is the only show where you come in at five A.M. and the producer says, "Can you come in earlier?" I'm here at five o'clock already; what do you want from me? ❞

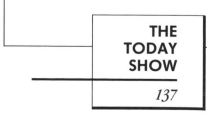

THE DIRECTORS

Sitting in the director's seat of *Today* since 1982 is George Paul. Upon meeting this slightly rotund man you instantly know that within his frame is a very compassionate, talented gentleman. Under pressure he remains one, although the adjectives he directs toward the monitors and through the earphones are sometimes ungentlemanly. (The scenic picture of New York behind the *Today* desk was taken by George Paul, a multi-talented man.)

George Paul, director, at the console

Steve Friedman:

❝ George Paul is a man made for a program like this. Live television is his element. He can do news, he can do music, he can stay in the control room eight hours a day. This is a marriage between man and program. There is not a better live television director than George Paul. He is meticulous. ❞

Sitting next to George in the control room or in George's seat when he is away is Steve Rosen. Off and on the show for fourteen years, and full time since 1982, he provides a good balance for George, who he describes in one word—"Sensational." Steve keeps a low profile and wears loud socks.

Jeff Hark:

❝ Running the show is a concerted effort. I think Marty has for the longest time consistently put in the longest hours and has worked the hardest to put the show on the air every day. He and George are the two that really put the show on—day in and day out. Cliff [Kappler] is now involved. He came back from doing specials a year ago. Marty and George are the guys that really put it on the air. They get a lot of help from the writers, researchers, and everyone who put all the little pieces together. Then they get the big pieces. ❞

TODAY'S *RIGHT ARM*

In the fifties, the entire coast-to-coast *Today* staff probably numbered not much more than a hundred. Now that number is surpassed by the New York office alone, which employs over 125 people. With *Today* staffs based around the United States and the world, the original number is multiplied many times over. Although there are many *Today* bureaus all contributing to the totality of the show, Washington, Chicago, Los Angeles, and London are the four main limbs of *Today,* Washington being the right arm.

Since that very first telecast in 1952, the Washington office has been a vital and enthusiastic contributor and participant in *Today.* Whether part of the bureau six months, five years, seven years, or twenty years, the Washington staffers' dedication, involvement, and total support of *Today* are evident.

When someone says, "Life is a series of compromises. Personally, there is nothing I can't do; only things I haven't tried," you know that person is a leader and you hope you will be on the same team. The quote is from Margaret Lehrman, the soft-spoken, efficient, Washington producer of *Today.*

Margaret Lehrman:

Margaret Lehrman, Washington producer

❻ Because ours is a morning program, we often have to awaken people when news is breaking to invite them to be on the air. These overnight calls can be very revealing.

On election night 1980, when the Senate shifted from a Democratic to a Republican majority, I woke up Senate Republican leader Howard Baker to tell him of the shift and that he could be the new Senate leader. His reaction: unprintable.

One morning of breaking news, I called Senator Claiborne Pell at home. He was about to fly to Europe and was harried and rude. A few days later, he sent a note of apology.

Sometimes because we want to contact needed guests first, we are the first to inform them of a dramatic event. I was first to reach the Indian Ambassador with news of Indira Gandhi's assassination. I

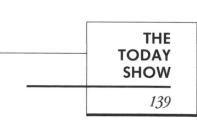

THE
TODAY
SHOW

also insisted on awakening Lebanon's ambassador so that I could tell him of the bombing of the American embassy in Beirut.

After I spent weeks, on my own initiative, to obtain an interview for Chris Wallace with Ann Haldeman, daughter of H. R. Haldeman, the morning dawned. Ann arrived with her roommate. She hadn't slept much, and she was nervous. We talked and laughed, and she relaxed some. But when she and Chris went on the air, Ann froze. Chris tried several questions, and she simply froze. In the control room, I was dying. It seemed like four years passed by. Finally, Chris leaned forward, patted Ann on the arm, and said gently, "It's okay. It's just you and me sitting here having a conversation." The interview sailed on. I breathed again. And Chris got tons of mail because viewers saw a side ❜ of him they hadn't seen before.

Max Schindler, Washington director

Washington news director Max Schindler has been in the bureau for over twenty years.

Max Schindler:

❛ I was in Minneapolis the morning after the election in November 1964 in a mobile unit outside the Radison Hotel. I spotted the new vice-president-elect, Hubert H. Humphrey, coming out and quickly asked him if he would do an interview on the *Today* show. None of the other networks were there. He said yes. I went into the mobile unit and told the *Today* control to put us on the air, that we had the vice-president-elect. They said I would have to wait five minutes as it was seven twenty-five A.M. That's when local stations cut away and do five minutes of local news. I went back outside and told Humphrey, thinking to myself that he would leave. He surprised me and said he would wait. Moral: Be careful what you ask for, you ❜ might get it—and be prepared.

Paul Cunningham, Today *reporter, interviewing Hubert H. Humphrey*

Margaret Lehrman:

❛ Working in Washington sometimes allows access to information that should not be broadcast—not the personal stuff but the sensitive information that has to be safeguarded. It has to be handled very carefully because it literally could mean a matter of life and death.

During the four hundred forty-four days that our hostages were in Iran, there was a time when we had six who were in the Canadian embassy, which I had known for several months. The secret was kept until they were safely out. **9**

Kathy Filosi Nelson has been with the Washington Bureau five years. Originally a writer for Chris Wallace, she then worked with Ken Bode as producer for his "Journal" and is now a field producer working with various correspondents in Washington and around the country.

Kathy Filosi Nelson:

6 The *Today* show has always been on top for me. When I was little, around five or six, I started going with my parents to New York every year. I *had* to do three things—go to Radio City, eat at Mama Leone's, and wave at Dave Garroway and Muggs at Thirty Rock! My mother always had a crush on Garroway and broke down in tears when I got this job. We had come full circle.

I remember my very first story with Ken Bode. In fact, it was the first time I had ever been in the field to produce *anything*—I had had plenty of studio experience, but as far as getting out there with a crew and telling them what to do, forget it! Thank God Bobby de Servi from Chicago was my cameraman. He literally took me by the hand those three days and became my mentor. This story involved a kid named Eric Salem who ran for and was elected at the age of thirteen to the post of county weed commissioner in Lincoln, Nebraska. It was a tough first shoot because we decided to do an interview with the head of the commission in a swampy weed field, as he pointed out all the leafy spurge! It was September, the temperature was in the nineties, and the mosquitos were about the size of dwarf hippos. There I learned the chief function of a field producer was to keep the mosquitos away from the cameraman so he could be steady and to *try* to keep them off the correspondent so that he could look presentable. This left very little time to keep myself from being chewed alive!

That night, after soaking in calamine lotion, the

crew, Ken, and I went to dinner, where I learned my second lesson of the road—never order fish where you can't see the water. After dinner, we decided to go down to the University of Nebraska in Lincoln, home of Big Red, the number-one football team in the country, and have some fun. We set up the camera in front of the student union about ten-thirty. It was the first week of school, and there were lots of folks milling about. Ken proceeded to go on camera to announce—in front of many students standing around us—that we had just left a meeting of the University Board of Regents where they had announced that they were dropping the football program, effective immediately, in favor of a nursing school. Hysteria broke out up and down fraternity row. Students came on camera crying, to express shock and disbelief. We explained it was just part of a gag reel, and then we left—quickly!

We went up to Minnesota and South Dakota to do a "Journal" on the "Boader War" going on between the two governors up there, a crazy dispute over which state was better. It was the middle of the winter, and Ken and I caught a flight out of Washington to Minneapolis/St. Paul, where we were to catch a connecting flight to Hibbing, Minnesota. The crew—de Servi again—was to pick us up in Hibbing. Travel being what it is in the Midwest in the winters, our flight was delayed, and we got to our connecting gate just as they were retracting the jetway. We had to be in Hibbing the next morning, so Ken chartered a flight while I got our bags. The plane was a six-seater with two pilots. One was about ninety and hard of hearing; he was flying the plane. The other was a young guy I *wish* had been flying the plane! I hadn't flown in many small planes at that point. We flew over *nothing* for one and a half hours and, twinkling in the distance, we saw a few lights. Ken nudged me. "Hibbing," he said. "Terrific," I said.

We landed on an air strip with a quonset hut at the end. I waited in the plane, while Ken and the old guy went to the phone booth to call a cab. Ken was in the phone booth and the guy was standing outside. It was a bad connection to Information and Ken was yelling into the receiver, "Yes, a cab company in Hibbing, we need a cab." The operator was confused and then, all of a sudden, the old guy started banging on the door yelling, "Mister! This isn't Hibbing, this is Bemidji." We finally got to Hibbing two hours later, with the pilot commenting all the while on how he couldn't understand why we wanted to go to Bemidji in the first place! **"**

Margaret Lehrman:

" I booked a guest everyone went crazy over. A Thai. His name was Mechai Viragaidya. He is Mr. Birth Control in Thailand. He came into our control room and passed out panties with MECHAI written on them. MECHAI is stamped on everything. In Thailand, if a family is practicing birth control, they can get a discount on leasing a water buffalo to plow their rice fields. On the side of the water buffalo it says MECHAI. Mechai underwear is often on the clotheslines. **"**

Entertainers are not alone with their narcissistic tendencies. Some *Today* insights into political vanity: a congressman who always wears mascara, a senator who asked about a particular brand of

Ted Kennedy getting ready to go on the air

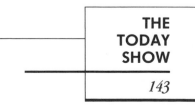

THE
TODAY
SHOW

143

eyeliner and blusher and left wearing both, a former Democratic Cabinet official who weaves one long strand of hair around his head to make it look like more, and a Republican senator who spits on his hands to set his hair in place.

Margaret Lehrman:

❝ Working in Washington is exciting, meeting presidents, heads of state, administration and congressional leaders, as well as entertainment figures. Some of these people are asses; some are just human; and some are caring, wonderful people.

One morning our makeup artist had to bring in her one-year-old, and then-Treasury secretary Donald Regan sat and fed him cereal. Incidentally, after Regan's twenty-fifty appearance on our program, we presented him with a *Today* windbreaker, that says SECRETARY DON, which he wears sailing.

We are often in the control room for six hours at a stretch. Tensions do exist. One morning we had been doing back-to-back interviews almost nonstop. When it was all over and we had nothing to do, the audio man put on "We Are the World" and we all started dancing. ❞

THE VIEWER FAMILY

Joe Garagiola:

❝ When I got up in the middle of the night to do *Today*, there would be streaks when I'd get absentminded because I'd get so involved in what I was doing. For instance, the only two rings I wear are my World Series ring and my wedding ring. I wear my wedding ring on my left hand and my World Series ring on my right. When I go to sleep I take them off. Well, I had a streak there when I forgot to put the rings back on, and I got mail from people wanting to know if I was having problems at home. It is more than being observant—the *Today* viewers' families are into the *Today* family.

My mother died while I was in Miami. I wasn't on the show and they said why I wasn't, that I had gone to St. Louis. The outpouring of mail and condolences was unbelievable. I guess it is because most people watching the show are in some form of disarray—they are either in their housecoats or curlers, or don't have any makeup on, or are feeding children. But you come in every day, and you become part of their family, you really do. They really take you in, and when they ❞ do they are very loyal.

THE STAFF

Over the past thirty-five years thousands of people have worked on the *Today* show. But what is it like to be part of *Today* now? An outsider can describe impressions, conversations, and interactions while in the office or the studio of *Today,* but those are only from the vantage point of an observer, not a daily participant. What *Today* is really like can accurately be described only by the people who are there hour by hour, day by day.

As with any successful organization, there are many different kinds of people participating in *Today* on many different levels and capacities.

Steve Friedman:

❦ I hire people for what I think of their brains, what I think of them as persons. I do not look at tapes. No one ever gives you a bad tape. I don't look at résumés; no one ever gives you a bad one. You can't tell anything from them. Recommendations don't matter either. Most people are nice. What I do is I talk to people to see what they are like and then I ask them to look at the show. I ask them to critique it, what they thought of it, what they liked and didn't like and how they would change it. I hire mostly based on how I feel about them—gut reactions. I want a certain type of individual.

Everyone must feel a part of the show, even if they had nothing to do with it. I also look for people who are killers. When I say go and get that done, when I say get that person, I don't want to hear, "I tried." Trying doesn't mean anything. You better go and get them. It is very straightforward. Don't give me that baloney, "I tried." I am not interested in people who try, I am interested in people who deliver. We all try. The ❦ German army tried.

Nancy Fields *(production assistant):*

❦ Steve transformed the show. He had the good sense to bring in the necessary people and put them in the right place, especially women. He also announced, "I want everyone on this show to have a good time!"

Kay Bradley's title is program manager. But that does not describe enough of what she does. She keeps it all running, hiring and firing staff, and acting as den mother. Inhabiting a purple office, her "den," Kay manages everything in a firm, pleasing, and efficient fashion. Steve Friedman says, "She's my boss. I do what she says." Really? "Absolutely!"

Researchers are vital to a "spot" on the show. Kay Bradley has said, "Researchers are the foundation of a spot. They get whatever is necessary."

Rosemarie Barone (senior researcher):

Assembling research, pre-interviewing guests, shooting stories in the field, screening footage, editing material for anchors, I'm a Jack of all trades.
I was sent to Washington to get a Cuban political prisoner as a guest on the *Today* show. Jesse Jackson and his Cuban refugee flotilla weren't arriving until four A.M. I spent nearly ten hours waiting at the airport with family members, being filled in on twenty-three years of emotions. I became one of the family. The most touching moment was being part of the tearful reunion between a husband and wife, separated for twenty-three years, and watching all the years melt away. They seemed like newlyweds.

Before becoming a researcher, **Ann Schlitt** was Jane Pauley's assistant for over five years. She handled the job with diplomatic aplomb, enthusiasm, and graciousness and learned not to make assumptions about folks based on their job titles.

Hilary Kayle is a senior researcher who has been with *Today* since October 1976. She began her career with the show as a receptionist. Over the years she has traveled thousands of miles with the show and has met many legendary figures from the worlds of politics, music, theater, and art. Her experiences often have been accented with twinges of panic, as when Bryant Gumbel's and NBC Vice-President Gordon Manning's luggage was lost for six hours in Moscow. Or going with Jane to a restaurant in

Hilary Kayle, senior researcher

Tokyo where no one spoke English. There have been many stress-free highlights as well, like meeting Paul Newman, Placido Domingo, and Richard Burton. But one experience that has a special personal meaning was the day Hilary put aside her researcher duties and performed on *Today* with her chamber chorus and Peter, Paul and Mary.

Many researchers begin as receptionists in the *Today* office, where they learn the comings and goings of people and the general rhythm of the office.

Barbara Lyons began her *Today* career just that way, then moved on to become a production assistant, then researcher for the book coordinator, and is now researcher for the talent department.

Barbara Lyons:

Once Robert Redford called to speak to Tom Brokaw, and I said, "Really? I'm sure you can come up with something better than that."

The writers put together what the researchers have gleaned from their research. Some mornings, with last-minute changes in formats taking place, the writer will still be preparing a script scant minutes before air time.

There are two categories of writers—program writers and newswriters.

Paul Brubaker (program writer):

To work on *Today* is alternately fulfilling and a tease limited only by one's imagination and energy and the fact that segments are only five minutes long. The closer you get to a story, the harder it is to be satisfied with the limitation imposed by five minutes.

A newswriter with *Today* for over fourteen years, Ray Smith has written a lot of news. He says that the newswriters are "*Today*'s forgotten staff."

Some *Today* staffers have been with the show since the sixties. **Doreen Jagoda** is not only one of those veterans but was also one of *Today*'s first woman writers. The show was totally different then—the staff was small, you had an enormous amount of responsibility, and, as Doreen says, "You really learned the business."

Doreen Jagoda (writer):

Al Morgan was the producer. I was sent to Greece all by myself to book the people, line up the program, and set the show. It was a fantastic experience. I learned by doing. The *Today* show gave me the opportunity to meet the achievers and feel their energies and goals. Working on the show now, I am probably the happiest I have ever been, although it is very different from those early unstructured days— now everything is well organized.

For Doreen and a few other staff members who have been with the show since the early days, it is probably hard to discern where one's *Today* life stops and where one's private life begins, or vice versa. Their coexistence makes for a challenging as well as rewarding experience.

Kathleen Graham (publicist):

I heed my mother's advice—"There's always humor in any situation, and if you can find it, it's probably the only thing that can keep you sane." *Today* is hectic, but fun. It has to be fun and invigorating, otherwise why would all these supposedly intelligent, well-educated people get up in the middle of the night over a thirty-four year period? It's also a little unnerving since, as publicist, I have to keep up on current events, sports, and entertainment gossip so I can keep a handle on everything going on on the show.

Art director **Carole Lee Carroll**'s creative touches can be seen in the attractive *Today* sets. On hand at six each day to give artistic direction on setups for the next morning—such as arrangements of items on counters for demonstration segments—Carole's philosophy of working on *Today* is, "Prepare for the unexpected at all times."

Piera De Michele and Carol Di Branco

Tammy Brown, assistant to the executive producer

Gloria Louise Casanovas, coffee lady

Nancy Fields, a production assistant, has been with *Today* for many, many years. She began as Al Morgan's secretary and since then has traveled with the show through all of its peaks and valleys. She currently works with Willard Scott and Joe Witte.

Transportation arrangements, hotel reservations, limo services are vital details of the daily *Today* routines and the prerequisites for handling them are patience and organization. The two production assistants who have those qualities are **Piera De Michele** and **Carol Di Branco.** Their smiles and cheery dispositions far outweigh the growls that their job often provokes.

Tammy Brown is assistant to the executive producer. Tammy handles her challenging job with aplomb. The number of people desiring an appointment with *Today*'s executive producer would fill pages of a New York phone book, but all the calls, lunch dates, trips, itineraries, and appointments are skillfully handled by this determined, goal-oriented young woman. She is impressed at how the show operates in pressure situations, but it is impressive how calm she is under pressure.

Keeping coffee urns filled, water for tea available, packets of tea, Sanka, and sugar substitutes, pitchers of cream and milk and trays full of pastries has been handled by Gloria Louise Casanovas for almost fifteen years. Weary staffers are always happy to see her.

SECURITY

In 1952, when *Today* could be viewed through the windows of the RCA Exhibition Hall, security was not a prime issue. It was a term reserved for potentates, political and military officials, Brinks deliveries, and Oscar nominations. Now it is a part of our daily lives in airports, in department stores, in offices, and at the *Today* show.

The NBC security force is always on the job. They are there to direct, protect, and lend a feeling of safety. The feeling is it is better to have it and not need it than to need it and not have it.

Many of the guests on *Today* receive the ultimate security treatment. They arrive by limousine at a specific time. They are met and greeted by an assigned *Today* show staff member. In matters of highest priority, a staff member and an empty elevator are waiting to usher the dignitary to the studio, where a special private room is waiting.

Recently, security was at its tightest for a particular guest. A security sweep of the studio was done. During the local news break, everyone evacuated the studio. Security officers, along with specially trained dogs, scrutinized the premises. The furniture, the piano—everything—was examined. The crew was thoroughly but quickly checked, then allowed to return. The guest was escorted in, interviewed, and clandestinely escorted out via a secret route.

Another form of security is when a guest does not want his face shown to the viewers. When this occurs, the guest is shot in shadow or from behind, or wears a mask. On a recent segment about cocaine addiction masks were used on several businessmen who did not want to be seen.

Margaret Lehrman:

❝ Trained security dogs often go through the Washington studios. We are used to security checks. We once had lockers outside the control room and everytime the dogs would go past them they would go bonkers. It turned out only to be something in the gaffers' tape that set them off. ❞

The Washington studios of *Today* are frequently visited by the Secret Service, particularly when the vice-president, the chief of staff,

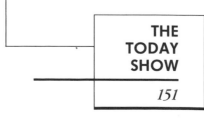

or the secretary of state are on the show. High security measures are also in effect when ambassadors are to appear, the tightest being for the Israeli ambassador.

Margaret Lehrman:

❝ There have been incidents in the Washington studio. We had one of the Contra leaders from Nicaragua on one morning and we received a phone call in the control room saying two reporters were coming over. That's the kind of stuff that throws up a red flag to us right away. We don't let them in the building because we would not jeopardize the guest in any way. ❞

Hilary Kayle:

❝ For my first five years on the show I was part of the early shift that is there to greet guests and take them to makeup. I was pretty experienced at doing this, but one morning I got off the elevator and there were these Secret Service people every ten feet or so along the hallway. And I thought, What is going on? I had looked at the guest list the night before and there was nothing that indicated there was going to be anyone special on the show. I walked into the Green Room and there was Moshe Dayan. He was so nice, so friendly. But again we were surrounded by guards, and I realized the threat of terrorism had prevented any advance notice of his appearance. When I got in the room, they closed the door. There I was with Moshe Dayan, two guards on the inside, and two just outside the door. It was a strange and almost terrifying feeling, but what was ironic about it was that he was so nice, so thoughtful, and charming, even with all this entourage. Over the years I had been with several heads of state, but no one had ever closed the door. It was a strange feeling that revealed how potentially dangerous it was to be in his presence. ❞

Nancy Fields:

❝ One day we got a call from a young man saying he had a letter of recommendation from his university and, since he was studying television production, could he visit the show? That afternoon he brought the letter and I showed it to the producer. He said, "Sure, put his name on the approved list for the morning." The next day I was watching the show when suddenly there were unexpected loud noises and cameras being knocked about. What happened was the guy had stolen the stationery. He was involved with the gay rights movement and was annoyed not so much with the *Today* show but NBC's coverage of the issue and **9** wanted to get some attention.

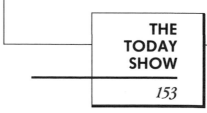

The Green Room

THE GREEN ROOM

The Green Room is the room in which a guest waits before appearing on a show. The *Today* Green Room is almost directly in front of the guest who arrives in the *Today* show hallway. The room is usually filled with other guests sitting on the oversized beige sofas or standing around. They will be talking or watching the show on the television in front of the sofa. Voices rollercoaster up and down. There are usually too many people for a room its size. Gene Shalit often comes in to have his guest sign or draw in his personal guest book. Celebrity pictures are on the wall. In the corner is a table with coffee, tea, and a box of pastries. Morning newspapers are within reach. Staff members are on hand to guide, soothe, get signed releases, and smile.

In the Washington *Today* Green Room, which actually *is* a pale green, a lot of protocol is in effect. An effort is made to make sure that people are introduced to one another even if they won't be on together.

Margaret Lehrman:

❝ We have guests who will not sit in the Green Room together—people who are coming on the same show, but who will not put themselves in the same room beforehand. They don't want anything to do with each other. They want to make their case on the air and let it go at that, so we have to put them in different rooms. ❞

Dorothy Lissner (Evins) (commercial producer):

Dorothy Lissner (Evins), commercial producer

❝ I met my husband in the Green Room. He was a guest on the show. It was his first TV interview and he was nervous. I was not supposed to be working that morning, but the previous night someone asked me to cover for them.

I sat with him and talked for a half hour before air time to prepare him and help stop the nervousness. He was great on the air. After the show he sent me a long-stemmed rose and a thank-you note. He asked me out for the next week and we got married in September 1985. I believe I'm the only staff member to have met my spouse this way. **9**

Hilary Kayle:

6 I love music and to be in the Green Room having Pinchas Zukerman and Itzhak Perlman both there rehearsing was incredible. They were so attuned to each other. I call this a perk. If you are going to get up at five in the morning, **9** this is not a bad way to begin the day.

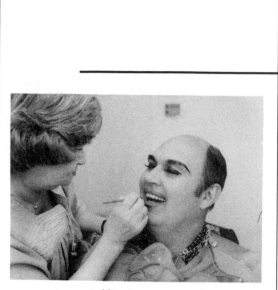

*Bobbie Armstrong, makeup artist—
making up Willard*

ALONG THE HALLWAY

Barbara "Bobbie" Armstrong has been hiding wrinkles and circles under the eyes and taking the shine off the faces of *Today* cast members and guests for over twenty-five years. With her slightly stern morning expression she'll say, "Come on, hon, let me make you up." Or she will greet the highest dignitary with a short "Good morning."

Bobbie will not readily give unsolicited advice. She lets you know in her own way and if you're smart you'll listen. It is more like her to say, "Are you wearing that sleeveless sweater? Unless you have toothpick arms that sleeve length is difficult to wear."

Barbara Walters:

❝ Bobbie Armstrong has been there forever. She's wonderful. You know, when I came here [ABC], it was very hard. I was in agony, and Bobbie would do the *Today* show in the morning and then she would come over here to do me in the afternoon because it was a solace for me to have her do my makeup. ❞

Katherine Gordon is the hairstylist. From the instant a guest walks into the makeup room she is studying that person's hair. She has but a few minutes to do what takes hours in the beauty salons. She'll ask, "How do you want your hair?" or "What are we going to do today?" and gets the guest coiffed quickly and expertly.

Grace Sicignano has been head of wardrobe for twenty years. She mends, tends, and pins the wardrobes of the cast and gives helpful suggestions about style: "That blouse is too busy. Did you bring something else? You need a pin on the blazer lapel. Let me get the wrinkles out. Keep the jacket on, but push up the sleeves."

The *Today* studio has changed locations over the years. From the RCA Exhibition Hall, with its famous window, *Today*'s cameras, cables, telephones, microphones, maps, clocks, and newspapers have been in studios 3K, 8H, 6B, and 8G, and are now at home on the third floor, in Studio 3B. But what has remained constant is the magical aura of the *Today* show studio. On-air or off, the atmosphere there exudes television at its best. "Firsts" of all varieties—animal, vegetable, mineral, rich, poor, prominent, convicted, humorous, sad, mundane, important—have at one time or another all emanated from within the *Today* studio.

Stage managers are in charge of all that happens in the studio and are in constant communication with the control room. It is their job to see that the talent gets to and from the right place at the right time. They give the time cues and when they make a fist, they aren't saying, "put up your dukes," they're signaling to wrap it up. Airtime is up.

Jim Straka has been a stage manager with *Today* for over twenty years. With his crew cut and casual attire, he convincingly consoles and cajoles the guests.

Jim Hartz:

❝ Straka is super. He is a guy who doesn't trouble you with needless information. He really knows the show. ❞

Mark Traub, the younger stage manager, also knows how to handle crew, staff, and guests and executes his job with authority. His pet peeve is noise in the studio—it could cost him his job.

Stephen "Steve" Bellis, cameraman, has been an essential part of *Today* for over eighteen years. To him, *Today* is "rough, interesting, never a dull moment." Steve says one of the greatest moments of his life was in 1975 when he appeared on *Today* as a performer. "I sang two original compositions. I was interviewed by Gene Shalit. This happened because Stuart Schulberg [then the producer] heard me singing in the hallway."

Good cameramen are important. They shoot guests from the best angles and can focus on something else if there is a goof somewhere on the set.

Bernie Florman has been with the *Today* show since 1959, as property manager. Many have termed him the Miracle Worker. He knows how to get things done and if he doesn't know (a rare occurrence), one can be sure he probably knows someone who does.

Segment preparation

Jim Straka and Mark Traub, stage managers

Bernie Florman:

💬 Those early days were something else. God, we had a good time. We were a very close knit group.

I remember one time in Puerto Rico. Jim Gaines was the producer. He was always asking me to get him milk. He had an ulcer. So I rented a cow and hung a sign on the cow saying "For Jim Gaines only." 💬

Hugh Downs:

💬 Bernie Florman is a genius. I never saw anybody as capable as Bernie at finding something that was almost impossible to get for an absurd hour of the morning. I remember one time someone decided we needed chickens hatching on the air. Can you imagine saying, "Get me chickens hatching"? Bernie contacted some guy he knew in New Jersey with a poultry nursery and he brought these eggs in and they hatched right on air!

Jack Lescoulie wanted a glass football—life size—to use as a crystal ball to gaze into to make some predictions. He told Bernie the night before. Lescoulie never thought he could get one. Bernie came up with a glass football. Asked how he did it, Bernie said, "I've got this old army buddy who knows a glassblower and he got him out of bed in the middle of the night and he blew the football."

There's never been anybody like Bernie Florman. I'm not kidding. He's unbelievable. 💬

Bernie knows how it *was* done, how it *is* done, and how it probably *will* be done.

Hubert Leufkens, known as "Bert," has been a propman/stage technician at *Today* "on and off for thirty-three years." Bert says, "With my partner, we handle the physical things such as scenery, curtains, furniture, displays, commercial items, and so forth." Bert is not hesitant to share a joke with a nervous guest or contributor, thereby easing the tension. "I've been in show business for so long that nothing surprises me," he says. But maybe it will before he retires in two years.

Hubert "Bert" Leufkens

GERRY DAVIS

158

WHAT IT'S REALLY LIKE

Studio 3B, with all its excitement, its hushed and frantic moments, its mishaps, its surprises, its serendipities, is where *Today* takes place. But what one sees is not all that is happening in Studio 3B.

Art Ulene:

Today is extremely rewarding. Not just for the activity itself, but for the amount of social good I'm able to do. I could practice five thousand years in a medical office and not have as much positive impact on people's lives.

Cynthia Samuels *(political producer):*

I have never worked in an environment like this in my life. There is a sense of teamwork that I find unduplicated. The level of dedication of people to their work at the *Today* show is amazing. Everyone likes it so much here, the turnover rate is minuscule.

Steve Friedman once said to me, "When somebody else's piece is bad, I want everybody to feel bad." Nobody ever gloats over anybody else's screw-up. People help each other out. People work insane hours to do the little extras to make it better. It is for the quality of the product, for making it the best it can be and having a great time doing it, because when you do it that well, it is fun—and that says a lot for the leadership.
It is the best job in the world.

Linda Ellerbee:

Today has been the show most amenable to experimentation of the regularly scheduled shows. Steve Friedman, and his theory of creative anarchy, have given me the freedom to push edges and to try new things. It's a very special combination of tradition and yet a place to experiment. It's a Montessori newsroom.

Cheryl Wells, researcher

David Naggiar *(senior unit manager):*

❝ Serving the *Today* show staff can be trying at times. Each one has his or her own little thing. Some are like babies, some are very professional. It's almost a twenty-four-hour job—hard to turn off when you go home. It's a thrill to be involved in something and see the product on the air ❞ and know that you had a part in it.

Cheryl Wells:

❝ I've been with the show four years. Oh, I love it, I love it. I can't believe they pay me to do this. It drives me crazy ❞ sometimes, but I love it.

Mark Traub:

❝ The effort of waking up in the cold, dark morning is rewarded daily on my arrival by the companionship of the crew and the talent. I am still star-struck after five years in the business, and the opportunity to work with these ❞ people still gives me a big thrill.

Mike Leonard:

❝ There is unparalleled creative freedom in the business of television news. Steve Friedman allows me to choose the topic, the location, the length, and format of the feature stories I do. The producers don't see it until it airs. Because of that free hand, I've been able to experiment with style and content. What I do, therefore, is considered different from the average TV fare. Before getting this job, I was used to getting reprimanded ❞ for daydreaming. Now I get paid to do it.

Morrison Krus:

❝ Exciting—to be closely associated with Willard Scott. The man has a lot of class. He could replace anyone on the staff within a minute's notice. That is more than I can say about myself. **9**

Eric A. Chasanoff:

6 Except for the hours, the best job I ever had. **9**

Kathy Filosi Nelson:

6 Probably my best training for my life with the *Today* show came when I was in school in Boston. I worked for two years at Mass General Hospital in the emergency ward as the nonmedical person. Things would go from *very quiet* to total chaos in a very short period of time, which is essentially how it goes on *Today*, and I love it. The staff is great and, especially with the traveling I do—before my daughter was born, I was on the road every week, now it is about once a month—it's really like having a large family, seeing old friends as I go around the country. The crews at the different bureaus make it special. **9**

Max Schindler:

6 It is exciting and challenging. We meet new people every day, different types of people. **9**

Margaret Lehrman:

6 It is never boring, in spite of the long hours. **9**

Tammy Brown:

6 It is exciting, challenging, frustrating, fulfilling, educational, and hectic. **9**

Bob Bazell:

6 My regular appearance on *Today* is the equivalent of a newspaper column for a television

journalist. I choose the subject and present it my own way. It has been an enormous opportunity for me which has allowed me to present all sorts of fascinating material that otherwise would not make it on to network television. **)**

Steve Bellis:

(It's rough, interesting, never a dull moment. **)**

Ray Smith:

(It's tiring. **)**

Hilary Kayle:

(It's hectic, exciting, challenging, creative, relentless. **)**

Rosemarie Barone:

(To quote Steve Friedman, it's "chaotic." Steve loves constant chaos, which promotes ideas, excitement, and energy for the show. I thrive on change; I'd die in a straight nine-to-five job where every day was the same as the next. Constant change keeps your mind challenged and ideas flowing. I love the travel, too. **)**

Dorothy Lissner (Evins):

(*Today* is unpredictable, challenging, fast paced, frustrating at times. But I wouldn't trade it for anything right now. **)**

Barbara Lyons:

(I don't think it's possible to find a better group of people to work with. It's a fun, creative, busy atmosphere—*especially* being on the road. **)**

Janice "J.J." DeRosa:

❻ This is one of the best jobs ever. When I go away on a remote I have to work twice as hard as I do here, but I don't care. I think everyone on the show gives one hundred percent because everyone likes it so much. And Steve makes you like it; you really want to do it for Steve. ❾

Mariann Murphy *(former assistant to Steve Friedman):*

❻ One day was never the same as the next. It was unusual, amusing, different, wonderful, awful, questionable, romantic, sensational, exciting. An unforgettable day was when Bill Cosby was a guest on the show. He was an absolute scream—he made my whole day. ❾

Don Haynie:

❻ I have worked on practically every show. The *Today* show is the most rewarding, but also the most demanding, with the longest hours. No one will every say "I love the *Today* show 'cause I get great hours." You can't get worse hours. ❾

Steve Friedman:

❻ I don't think you can work on the show unless you really like it. There are easier ways to make a living, and you don't have to get up at four every morning. You have to like what you are doing or you cannot get up to do it. Once you think of it as a job that is drudgery, it is time for you to get out. ❾

Tom Brokaw:

❻ There is another thing you become aware of when you do the *Today* show—and for me it is true even to this day—people come up to you and say, "Gee, I miss you on the *Today* show," or "I remember when you talked about your father retiring," or the day something happened with your children. More than anything else we do, there is a personal connection with the audience. It has to do with the time of day. You also let your guard down over the course of two hours, so the viewers get to know you on **99** very human terms.

A Tradition Continues

Before 1986 was over, the *Today* show had presented hundreds of stories and interviews. From the crisis in Libya to the nuclear disaster in Kiev; business reports, sports events, human interest stories, demonstrations of the phones of the future, tips on traveling with your children, catalog shopping, fashion predictions, life-style segments, and much, much more were seen on *Today*.

Aside from in-the-studio reports *Today* traveled . . . again. In May aboard the S.S. *Norway, Today* took its audiences to Wilmington, North Carolina, Charleston, South Carolina, Savannah, Georgia, Mayport Naval Base, Florida, and Miami. Among the topics covered during the week-long sail were: history of the great ocean liners, ship security, mysteries and legends of the Bermuda Triangle, piracy, drug smuggling, tattooing, and other segments on various aspects of the seas. Scenic tours were taken in the various ports, and although the *Today* audience was on land, there was no question that it had been an enjoyable cruise for all.

Steve Friedman:

❝ Out of all the trips, the cruise was the show's biggest undertaking. It was more ambitious than Rome because in Rome we were in the same city every day and you had a regular life. On the train we just basically got off ❞ the train and did a show.

From on the sea to across the sea, in July *Today* went to London to cover the Royal Wedding of Prince Andrew and Sarah Ferguson.

There was no doubt about it, 1986 had been an eventful year. But then there had been many eventful years for *Today* and there was also no doubt that there would be many more. *Today*'s lot in life is to be the presenter of the eventful.

Steve Friedman:

❝ When you "run" this show you have custody of an institution. It is not my show, it is in my custody for however long it takes. It is not Jane's show,

it is not Bryant's show, it is in our custody. What we try to do is make our tenure—our time with the show—a time that it thrives, prospers, and changes so the next generation when they come along have a viable thing to work with. We are trying to stay truthful to the Dave Garroway–Pat Weaver format, which is for people to wake up and 9 find out what is going on in the world.

Tom Brokaw:

6 I don't think you can fully appreciate the *Today* show until you are away from it. You get consumed by the work. It is so consuming. *Today* is really a place of privilege . . . unlike 9 anything else in television news.

THIRTY-FIVE YEARS LATER

Out of the confusion and clutter of the early *Today* shows came a format that has changed very little over the years. *Today*'s news is presented on the half hour four times each morning and is always followed by a national weather report. At 7:25 and 8:25 affiliates across the country report their local news before the national news.

The 7:00 to 7:25 segment is primarily hard news stories. The 7:30 to 8:00 segment has pertinent stories of a more general nature. One can usually hear a debate of some timely topic from 8:00 to 8:25 and the 8:30 to 9:00 segment is usually devoted to entertainment and life-style presentations.

Jack Lescoulie (1952):

❧ **And we are going to bring you the great stories in the news just as often as we possibly can on this program—over your breakfast table, just as regularly as coffee is served.** ❧ **Wire photos will also be shown.**

Today is a place for discussion of public affairs, ideas, political viewpoints and concepts. It has presented music of all tempos, art of all mediums and people of all varieties. Rich, poor, destitute, criminal; politicians, celebrities, sportsmen, courtiers, doctors, lawyers, Indian chiefs; babies, youngsters, girls and boys; women and men who have lived the molds and also those who have broken molds; all types, all shapes and from all walks of life. Successes, failures, dreams; medical subjects, inventions, creations, realities and fantasies, there is not much that has not been presented in the 9,100 shows of *Today*. If an accurate tally had been kept of the number of guests appearing on *Today* over all the years, the number would probably be close to 50,000. Topics have been discussed, argued, considered, provoked, refuted, and settled. A lot, too, have just been left.

In 1952, the *Today* show was budgeted at $40,000 per week. In 1986, the *Today* show was budgeted at $720,000 per week and declared by many television critics to be one of the most influential shows in the history of television.

Early Today *studio in chaos*

Italian fashion show

With over 18,200 broadcast hours *Today* celebrates its thirty-fifty anniversary. *Happy* thirty-fifth!

Steve Friedman:

❝ What I think we will have in the next couple of years is a lot of experimentation within the basic format. I view the *Today* show as a television laboratory. You push technology, as fast as you can. You don't just sit there. ❞

Dave Garroway (1952):

❝ And right around the corner, now, is that coaxial cable or that big, big antenna that will make live programs between nations an ordinary event. But that's tomorrow. ❞

Mr. Garroway, your tomorrow has come, it is *Today*.

Mr. Weaver, Mr. Garroway, NBC, and all concerned since have taken the viewers to Rome, to Paris, to England. *Today* has gone across North America, visited Brazil and Argentina, returned to Europe, and plans to go to Australia. There is nowhere that is not "right around the corner" for *Today*.

One cannot predict what *Today*'s tomorrow will be—who the producers will be, the co-hosts, the contributors, the sponsors, the staff, what the budget will be, or what the ratings will be.

But the past is etched—or, more accurately for *Today*—processed on film or tape. It is there to look at, learn from, laugh at, and be in awe of. *Today* has done what it was originally created and designed to do.

EXCELLENCE ONCE ACHIEVED ENDURES.

PEACE

Pretzel twist group

Early studio

Gerry Davis has been associated with the *Today* show for over five years and has created and presented on the air more than thirty-five segments on varied topics. She is also the author of *The Moving Experience.* She's a native New Yorker now living in Virginia.